First World War
and Army of Occupation
War Diary
France, Belgium and Germany

48 DIVISION
144 Infantry Brigade
Worcestershire Regiment
1/7th Battalion
1 January 1916 - 31 October 1917

WO95/2759/1

The Naval & Military Press Ltd
www.nmarchive.com
Published in association with The National Archives

Published by

The Naval & Military Press Ltd

Unit 10 Ridgewood Industrial Park,

Uckfield, East Sussex,

TN22 5QE England

Tel: +44 (0) 1825 749494

www.naval-military-press.com

www.nmarchive.com

This diary has been reprinted in facsimile from the original. Any imperfections are inevitably reproduced and the quality may fall short of modern type and cartographic standards.

© **Crown Copyright**
Images reproduced by permission of The National Archives, London, England, 2015.

Contents

Document type	Place/Title	Date From	Date To
Miscellaneous	1/7 Worcestershire Regt Jan Vol XI		
War Diary	Courcelles	01/01/1916	09/01/1916
War Diary	Courcelles Sheet 57.d. J. 29	10/01/1916	29/02/1916
Heading	1/7 Worcester Regt Vol XIII		
War Diary	Courcelles 57d. J 29	01/03/1916	05/03/1916
War Diary	Colincamps 57d. K 25 C.	06/03/1916	11/03/1916
War Diary	Colincamps	12/03/1916	14/03/1916
War Diary	In Trenches. 57d. K.34	15/03/1916	19/03/1916
Heading	48 1/7 Worcester Regt Vol 14		
War Diary		01/04/1916	30/04/1916
War Diary	Beauval	09/05/1916	15/05/1916
War Diary	Coigneux	16/05/1916	30/05/1916
War Diary	Trenches 57D K 17c. K23d	01/06/1916	01/06/1916
War Diary	Gezaincourt 57D. A 21d.	02/06/1916	03/06/1916
War Diary	Neuville	04/06/1916	12/06/1916
War Diary	Yureincheux.	12/06/1916	14/06/1916
War Diary	Mezerolles	15/06/1916	15/06/1916
War Diary	Coigneux	16/06/1916	30/06/1916
Heading	War Diary Of 7th Worcestershire Regiment. From 1st July, 1916 to 31st July, 1916. (Vol. July, 1916)		
War Diary	Coigneux	01/07/1916	01/07/1916
War Diary	J. 15.c.5.3	01/07/1916	01/07/1916
War Diary	J. 18.c	01/07/1916	02/07/1916
War Diary	Q. 20.b	10/07/1916	10/07/1916
War Diary	Q 22b	11/07/1916	15/07/1916
War Diary	Q 22b	03/07/1916	03/07/1916
War Diary	J. 18.c	04/07/1916	04/07/1916
War Diary	Coigneux	04/07/1916	14/07/1916
War Diary	Bouzincourt	14/07/1916	15/07/1916
War Diary	X. 8.c. 23	15/07/1916	17/07/1916
War Diary	Point.09	17/07/1916	18/07/1916
War Diary	Point. 85	19/07/1916	31/07/1916
War Diary	Surcamps	01/08/1916	08/08/1916
War Diary	Candas	09/08/1916	09/08/1916
War Diary	Puchvillers	10/08/1916	11/08/1916
War Diary	Forceville	12/08/1916	12/08/1916
War Diary	W.8.d	13/08/1916	13/08/1916
War Diary	X 2a 85	21/08/1916	22/08/1916
War Diary	57. D. Q.9.b. 9.3	01/09/1916	05/09/1916
War Diary	Bus-Les-Artois	05/09/1916	12/09/1916
War Diary	Amplier	13/09/1916	17/09/1916
War Diary	Le Meillard	18/09/1916	29/09/1916
War Diary	Ivergny	30/09/1916	30/09/1916
War Diary	Ivergny Halloy	01/10/1916	07/10/1916
War Diary	Fonquevillers.	08/10/1916	13/10/1916
War Diary	Humbercourt	14/10/1916	19/10/1916
War Diary	Ivergny	20/10/1916	26/10/1916
War Diary	57c. X 22.d.	26/10/1916	31/10/1916
Heading	War Diary of 1/7th Worcester Regt From 1st to 30th. Nov 1916 (Vol XX)		

War Diary	57.D. X 22d	01/11/1916	03/11/1916
War Diary	X 21.b	04/11/1916	05/11/1916
War Diary	58.a. 79	06/11/1916	07/11/1916
War Diary	Martinpuich	08/11/1916	09/11/1916
War Diary	X 22d	10/11/1916	18/11/1916
War Diary	M 22d 42	19/11/1916	20/11/1916
War Diary	M 28d 36	21/11/1916	23/11/1916
War Diary	X 16d 90	24/11/1916	28/11/1916
War Diary	X 21d	29/11/1916	30/11/1916
Heading	War Diary of 1/7th Worcestershire Regiment From 1st December 1916. to 31st December 1916 Volume 21		
War Diary	Trenches. (X. 21.b) Tr. 22.d B1	01/12/1916	05/12/1916
War Diary	57. D. X. 11. b.	06/12/1916	09/12/1916
War Diary	M. 21.d. 3b	10/12/1916	12/12/1916
War Diary	M. 22d. b1.	13/12/1916	14/12/1916
War Diary	X 12. C. 31	15/12/1916	16/12/1916
War Diary	Albert	17/12/1916	28/12/1916
War Diary	Millencourt	29/12/1916	29/12/1916
War Diary	Baizieux	31/12/1916	31/12/1916
Heading	War Diary of 1/7th Bn Worcestershire Regt. From 1st to 31st January 1917 (Volume XXII)		
War Diary	Baizieux	01/01/1917	08/01/1917
War Diary	Huppy	28/01/1917	28/01/1917
War Diary	Cerisy	29/01/1917	31/01/1917
Heading	War Diary of 1/7th Bn Worcestershire Regt. July 1st to July 28th 1917 (Vol XXIII)		
War Diary	Cappy	01/02/1917	01/02/1917
War Diary	Trenches	02/02/1917	09/02/1917
War Diary	Cappy	10/02/1917	17/02/1917
War Diary	Trenches	18/02/1917	26/02/1917
War Diary	Cappy	27/02/1917	28/02/1917
Heading	1/7th Bn Worcestershire Regiment War Diary for March 1917 Volume 24		
War Diary	Cappy	01/03/1917	03/03/1917
War Diary	In Trenches	04/03/1917	07/03/1917
War Diary	Cappy	08/03/1917	08/03/1917
War Diary	Support Trenches	17/03/1917	17/03/1917
War Diary	Trenches & Outposts	18/03/1917	18/03/1917
War Diary	Outpost Position	19/03/1917	20/03/1917
War Diary	Peronne	26/03/1917	29/03/1917
War Diary	Tincourt	30/03/1917	30/03/1917
War Diary	Saulcourt Wood	31/03/1917	31/03/1917
Heading	War Diary of 1/7th Bn The Worcestershire Regt From 1/4/17 To 30/4/17 (Vol XXIV)		
War Diary	Epehy	01/04/1917	03/04/1917
War Diary	Hamel	04/04/1917	04/04/1917
War Diary	Outpost Line	12/04/1917	13/04/1917
War Diary	In Camp.	14/04/1917	16/04/1917
War Diary	Hamel	17/04/1917	25/04/1917
War Diary	Hamel	05/04/1917	08/04/1917
War Diary	Outpost Duty.	09/04/1917	09/04/1917
War Diary	Villers-Faucon	10/04/1917	12/04/1917
Miscellaneous	Headquarters 144 Infy Bde	15/04/1917	15/04/1917
Miscellaneous	Tk 55 Headquarters 144 Infy Bde.		
Miscellaneous	Operations of 1/7 The Worcestershire Regt on 13 April 1917	13/04/1917	13/04/1917

Miscellaneous	8th Worcs.		
Miscellaneous	Operations of 1/7 Bn The Worcestershire Regt Against Gillemont Farm on 24/25 April 1917	24/04/1917	24/04/1917
Operation(al) Order(s)	144 Infy Brigade Order No. 174	24/04/1917	24/04/1917
Miscellaneous	O.O. No. 3 by Lt Col. F.M. Tomkenson Commdg 1/7 Bn the Worcestershire Regt.	24/04/1917	24/04/1917
Map	Sketch Map Showing Dispositions on Immediately on Passing Thro Villages.		
War Diary		06/04/1917	30/04/1917
Map			
Heading	War Diary of 1/7th Bn The Worcestershire Regt. 1st May to 31st May 1917 (Vol. XXVI)		
War Diary	Trenches	01/05/1917	01/05/1917
War Diary	Hamel	02/05/1917	12/05/1917
War Diary	Peronne	13/05/1917	13/05/1917
War Diary	Combles	13/05/1917	14/05/1917
War Diary	Morchies	15/05/1917	21/05/1917
War Diary	Front Line	22/05/1917	30/05/1917
War Diary	Fremicourt	31/05/1917	31/05/1917
Heading	War Diary of 1/7th Bn The Worcestershire Regt (T.F.) 1st June to 30th June 1917 (Vol. XXVII)		
War Diary	Fremicourt	01/06/1917	07/06/1917
War Diary	Left Brigade Resue.	08/06/1917	14/06/1917
War Diary	Beugny Morchies-Beaumetz Line	15/06/1917	22/06/1917
War Diary	Left Front of Right Bde.	23/06/1917	30/06/1917
Heading	War Diary of 1/7th. Bn The Worcestershire Regt (T.F) From 1st to 31st July 1917 (Vol. XXVIII)		
War Diary	Fremicourt	01/07/1917	03/07/1917
War Diary	Blairville	04/07/1917	20/07/1917
War Diary	Berles-Au-Bois	21/07/1917	23/07/1917
War Diary	Poperinghe	24/07/1917	26/07/1917
Heading	War Diary of 1/4th Bn The Worcestershire Regt T.F. From 1/8/17 to 31/8/17 (Vol XXIX)		
War Diary	Camp. A 29d	01/08/1917	06/08/1917
War Diary	Camp at A 27	07/08/1917	08/08/1917
War Diary	Camp at. A. 30 C. 71	09/08/1917	17/08/1917
War Diary	Canal Bank	18/08/1917	18/08/1917
War Diary	Reigersburg Camp	19/08/1917	24/08/1917
War Diary	Canal Bank	25/08/1917	27/08/1917
War Diary	Dambre Camp	28/08/1917	29/08/1917
War Diary	Schools Camp	30/08/1917	31/08/1917
Heading	War Diary of 1/7th Bn Worcestershire Regiment T.F. From 1st to 30th September 1917 (Vol XXX)		
War Diary	Schools Camp St. Janster Biezen	01/09/1917	17/09/1917
War Diary	Zutkerque	18/09/1917	30/09/1917
Heading	1/7th Worcestershire Regiment War Diary 1st October-31st October 1917 Volume XXXI		
War Diary	Flanders Zutkerque	01/10/1917	02/10/1917
War Diary	Vlamertigne Area.	02/10/1917	13/10/1917
War Diary	Brake Camp	03/10/1917	05/10/1917
War Diary	Dambre Camp	06/10/1917	09/10/1917
War Diary	Ypres Area	09/10/1917	13/10/1917
War Diary	Lens Area.	14/10/1917	14/10/1917
War Diary	Ligny St Flochel	14/10/1917	15/10/1917
War Diary	Villers Au Bois	16/10/1917	16/10/1917
War Diary	Neuville St Vaast	17/10/1917	20/10/1917

War Diary	Vimy	21/10/1917	29/10/1917
War Diary	Neuville St Vaast	29/10/1917	30/10/1917
War Diary	Mt St Eloi	31/10/1917	31/10/1917
Miscellaneous			

1/7 Worcestershire Regt.

Jan

Vol XI

INTELLIGENCE SUMMARY.

(Erase heading not required.)

Instructions regarding War Diaries and Intelligence Summaries are contained in F. S. Regs., Part II and the Staff Manual respectively. Title pages will be prepared in manuscript.

Place	Date	Hour	Summary of Events and Information	Remarks and references to Appendices
COURCELLES	Jany 1916 1		Bucks General Holiday. Officers played 8/Worcesters at Rugger at BUS, and were beaten by 2 goals. Varells performed 6 P.M.	
	2		Bucks Corps Working parties 350 men.	
	3		Relieved 4th Bn Oxford & Bucks in 'G' Section of Trenches.	
	4		Trenches. Sheet 57.D.N.E. (3rd part of) K.17.c.2.5 to K.93.c.3.3.	
	5		"	
	6		"	
	7		"	
	8		"	
	9		Relieved by 4th Oxford & Bucks in G Section of Trenches and moved to Bucks	
COURCELLES	10		Billets. Bn. for interior economy. Baths at SAILLY, and Church Reinforced.	
Sheet 57.D. I.29	11		14 B.H.BRIGHT. and 2/LT. R.P.EDWARDS proceed to III Army Trench Mortar School 2/LT LLOYD, BAXTER, FRANCIS, and BROWN join. CAPT CASSELS and 2/LT VALENTINE attached to Bn from 12th	
			Inspection by Brigadier – good turn out. Sanatoria Cup Match, 9th Worcesters beat 4th Gloucesters 3 goals to nil.	
	14		R.E. Working Parties 370 men. Concert 6-0 p.m.	

INTELLIGENCE SUMMARY.

(Erase heading not required.)

Place	Date	Hour	Summary of Events and Information	Remarks and references to Appendices
	Jan 1916.			
	15.		Relieved 4th Bn Coldstream Guards in G Section of trenches relief complete 7.30 p.m. Trenches (Sheet. K.17.D. NE (Sheets 3 + 4 parts of) K.17.c.2.5. to K.23.b.3.3) Quiet day.	{Appx}
	16		" " " "	
	17		" " " "	
	18		" " " "	
	19		Lt Col Harman to Hospital. Capt Tomkinson takes Command. Major Howe attached to Flying Corps.	
	20		Trenches. Good shooting by Lt Mountain on the front by request.	
	21		" Relieved by 1st Bucks Battalion in G Section of trenches. Relief complete at 9.30 p.m. Bn all returned to billets at 9.45 pm. Casualties one man wounded.	
COURCELLES	22.		Billets. Companies at disposal of OC Companies for interior economy.	
Sheet 57.D.	23.		" Church parade 10-30 a.m. Lt.Col. Harman off on 14 days sick leave to England. Capt Wood goes on leave.	
J.24.	24		Billets. Battn for the Bn. at SAILLY and thrash Herenfelew. Officers football match v 8th Worcesters (Cocoa) won 5-0. Corps Commander in COURCELLES + watched the match, performance by 4th Devils Dothis at 6.0 pm	

INTELLIGENCE SUMMARY.
(Erase heading not required.)

Place	Date	Hour	Summary of Events and Information	Remarks and references to Appendices
COURCELLES. Sheet 57.D. J.29.	Jany 1916. 25		Burrells lecture on Gas by III Army Chemical Adviser, followed by demonstration, no one gassed. Concert 6-15 p.m. final of inter Company series	
	26.		Reliefs Pit. Working parties as usual. Taking all except "C" Coy. Varsham Cup tie V 6th Gloucesters, very even game, ending with score 2-1 for them, but match is to be replayed as the referee played 20 minutes extra time without being aware of it. 2nd Inter Co. concert given by D. Co. 6-15 p.m.	
	27		Relieved Bucks Battalion in G Section of trenches. Relief complete 8.0 p.m. 8th Worcesters on our left, Dublin Fusiliers on our right.	
	28		Trenches. C.O. visited Bde. H.Q. 7.0 P.M. of 2nd S.M.J.A. Rifle making arrangements for proposed stunt. Gas alarm 7-15 p.m. started from 184 Brigade, found to be false, all alarm arrangements worked very satisfactorily. Official opinion from Division is that alarm was probably caused by fog, and chlorine of lime being used by Sanitary Police. Party for to-morrows stunt rehearsed operations and reconnoitred the ground.	

INTELLIGENCE SUMMARY.

(Erase heading not required.)

Place	Date	Hour	Summary of Events and Information	Remarks and references to Appendices
	Jany 1916 29		British Trenches. Quiet day. A preananged raid on German trenches in front of this Bde & Warwick Bde was fixed for 3 am on morning of 30th Jany. This Bn was ordered to create a diversion to attract enemy's attention from main operation to the place on the left. Accordingly at 2:40 am a party consisting of 2/Lt DELITTLE and 22 other Ranks of A Coy with a covering party consisting of Lt. W.R. PRESCOTT and 35 other ranks A Coy moved out to the old German wire running from single they Sail to SERRE Road through wire gaps cut in our own wire. 'A' to the left of the first barricade B & on the 2nd Barricade EAST of the SERRE ROAD. The covering party was placed facing a gap cut through the old German wire and all were in position ready at 3-0 am. The signal gun went off at 3.58 am and was immediately followed by the 2nd & 3rd Gloucester Batteries who were to open a barrage on the German second line opposite own party whilst own party were waiting they could hear the Germans working on their own wire close to the objective which was the German front at K.17.a.2.3. As soon as the signal gun went off our raiding & breaking parties moved swiftly forward. The German wiring party at once sic-enclosed their trench leaving coils of wire on the ground out side. 2/Lt LITTLE and 8 other men went straight at the wire & started cutting 5 in front Nos 7 & 8 in second they cut through twenty yards when came on	

INTELLIGENCE SUMMARY.

(Erase heading not required.)

Place	Date	Hour	Summary of Events and Information	Remarks and references to Appendices
	Jan. 1916 29		(Cont.) Concertina wire which held them up they were then about 10 yards from the German trench the men they cut at this Concertina were the worse it became to deal with as at this point the Germans were the worse right amongst them but did little damage (they must have been plain H.E. Bombs) our party then through volleys of rapid rifle bombs (25 in all) into the German trench and as she wire were impassable and the alarm had been given they retired considering their task completed the retirement was carried out in good order at 4:13 am the front parties were back with the covering party and at 4:30 am all were in the men were bitterly cold after lying out for one hour owing to difficulty experienced by G/Colonists in finding their way in the fog our party had to wait for them & experienced difficulty for that reason in removing the split pins from the bombs. Our field guns kept up a continuous fire and at 4-2 am our Howitzers also opened up. At about 4-15 am a flash lamp signal from the covering party to the F.O.O. in trench AUVERGNE caused the Field guns to drop on to the German front line the German reply both by Artillery & Machine Gun & rifle fire was very feeble it is thought that considerable casualties must have been caused by our grenades, seeing that the German	

INTELLIGENCE SUMMARY.

(Erase heading not required.)

Place	Date	Hour	Summary of Events and Information	Remarks and references to Appendices
	Jany 1916 29.		(Cont) Trench was crowded with the men just come in from the working party as well as the usual garrison. Ours were 3 men very slightly wounded by fragments from Grenades two of these returned straight to duty. b/Lt LITTLE and Sergt J. Parkes led the covering party very gallantly. Pte Stanley it is reported to have done very well. C.S.M. Oliver who was in charge of half the evening party took great care trouble with the arrangements beforehand. The Brigadier and the G.O.C. 48th Division expressed themselves as very pleased with the result of the enterprise.	
		30	Trench. Foggy day. Brigadier General Nicholson came to Bn HQ to congratulate Capt Tomkinson on last night's enterprise very foggy dark night making work almost impossible.	
		31	Trenches. Fog gone G.O.C. came at 11-0 am and went round parts of the trenches with the C.O.	

J Tomkinson
CAPT.
Comdg. 1/7th Bn. Worcestershire Regt.

INTELLIGENCE SUMMARY.

(Erase heading not required.)

Summaries are contained in F. S. Regs., Part II and the Staff Manual respectively. Title pages will be prepared in manuscript.

Place	Date	Hour	Summary of Events and Information	Remarks and references to Appendices
	1916			
	July 1		Trenches.	Miss Kells
	2		" Relieved by Bucks Battalion in G Section of Trenches, and returned to Billets at COURCELLES	
COURCELLES Sheet 57 d S.29	3		Billets COURCELLES. Companies at disposal of O.C Companies for cleaning and Baths at SAILLY.	
	4		Billets Companies at disposal of O.C. Companies. Group final FANSHAWE cup result. 7th Worcesters 4 6th Gloucesters 0	
	5		Billets inspected by Commanding Officer	
	6		" Working Parties and Church Services. B. of E. 10.0 a.m. R.C. 8.30 a.m. Nonconformists 11.30 a.m.	lost
	7		Billets Working Parties. Semi-final FANSHAWE cup. 7th Worcesters 2 goals K.E.H. 0 Companies at disposal of O.C Companies for bombing, company	
	8		" drill and Baths at SAILLY.	
	9		Working parties on R.E. Corps line and COURCELLES.	
	10		Battalion inspected by Brigadier. LT. J.E. JORDAN found dead in his bed at 7.30 a.m.	11. 12
	11		Funeral of 2/Lt J.E. JORDAN at LOUVENCOURT at 3.0 p.m. Capt. TOMKINSON attended funeral. LT. PRESCOTT in charge of firing party.	

INTELLIGENCE SUMMARY.

(Erase heading not required.)

Place	Date 1916	Hour	Summary of Events and Information	Remarks and references to Appendices
	February 12		Billets. Companies at disposal of O.C. Companies.	
	13		Relieved 8th Battalion E. Lancs. Regt. and 2 Companies 6th Bedfords 112th Inf. Bde in trenches between E.22.a.2.0. and E.16.a.5.3. relief complete 9.0 pm. Headquarters in FONQUEVILLERS. Transport & Qm Stores at SOUASTRE trenches.	wet
	14			
	15		Our right Company relieved by 1/7th R. Warwickshire Regt. Headquarters move to a point in HANNESCAMPS – FONQUEVILLERS road approx: at E.16.a.4.4. A Company came out from the left went in on the right taking over.! Company from 6th Gloucester Regt. line held by the Battalion approx E.22.R.5.4. to E.17.a.4.4.	
	16		G.O.C. Division visited trenches in the morning	
	17		Relieved by 8th Bn Worcestershire Regt. moved back to Bde Reserve in BIENVILLERS. 6 platoons remain in HANNESCAMPS as garrison.	
	18			
	19		Early morning raid by enemy on trench 55 (8th Worcesters) Working parties draft of 13 O.R. from Base. Working parties.	

INTELLIGENCE SUMMARY.

Summaries are contained in F. S. Regs., Part II. and the Staff Manual respectively. Title pages will be prepared in manuscript.

(Erase heading not required.)

Place	Date	Hour	Summary of Events and Information	Remarks and references to Appendices
	February 1916 29		Due to relieve 8th Worcestershire Regt. Relief cancelled, and whole Brigade relieved by 112th Brigade. This Battalion moved half to SAILLY. Brigade Headquarters took over our COURCELLES, half to SOUASTRE.	over

J.H. Jenkinson Major.

Comdg 1/7th Bn Worcestershire Regt.

Army Form C. 2118.

WAR DIARY
or
INTELLIGENCE SUMMARY.
(Erase heading not required.)

1/4 Worcester Regt.
Vol XIII

M.13

Summary of Events and Information	Remarks and references to Appendices

Billets in Courcelles.

Kings Own Regt in E Section (Centre of front K.34 to q.o. to K.29 c.9?
a 5.5) Relief complete 11 p.m. 6" R.S.R. on right. Bucams 10" Corps on Army.
Snow fall; condition in front line trenches very bad. 2 day relief decided upon.

Battern of H.Down relieved by Glosters Bar R.F.A. Relieved by 8" Worcesters. Relief
Bad relief due to inadequate supply of gum boots. Went to Bailleul Colincamps 5p.D. K25E. parties.

In SAILLY (5p0?q9) Relieved E" Worcesters in E Section with 3 Coys. Relief complete 10.15 pm.
6" Corps Q.o.E. Brigade visited trenches in the morning.

Headqrs. Relief complete 9.30pm. Back to Bar. Reg. Colincamps a.b in billets 10.30p.m.
and baths at Colincamps.

Baths at SAILLY.

Army Form C. 2118.

Miss Brown H?W(?) M.13

WAR DIARY
or
INTELLIGENCE SUMMARY.
(Erase heading not required.)

Instructions regarding War Diaries and Intelligence Summaries are contained in F. S. Regs., Part II. and the Staff Manual respectively. Title pages will be prepared in manuscript.

Place	Date	Hour	Summary of Events and Information	Remarks and references to Appendices
COURCELLES 57.D.J.29.	1916 1st Nov.		Billets.	
	2nd "		Bn. closed up to Billets in Courcelles.	
	3rd "		Relieved 1st Bn. Kings Own Regt. in E Section (Control of Front K.3.u 4.9.0. to K.29 c.5.?) Bn. HQrs at K.3.u a.5.5.) Relief complete 11 p.m. Became 10th Corps in Army Trenches. Heavy snow fall; condition in front line trenches very bad. 2 day relief decided upon.	
	4th "		Supporting Battalion of "D" Divn. relieved by Gloster Bn. R.F.A. Relieved by 8th Worcesters. Relief complete 1.10 a.m. Bad relief due to inadequate supply of guru boots. Went to Bar Res. Colincamps 57.D. N.25.T.	
COLINCAMPS 57.D. N.25.C.	5th " 6th "		Bar Res. Working parties.	
	7th "		"D" Coy. to billets in SAILLY (Sp.O.9.g.) Relieved 6th Worcesters in E Section with 3 Coys. Relief complete 10.15 p.m.	
	8th "		Trenches. Became 6th Corps. G.O.C. Brigade visited trenches in the morning.	
	9th "		In trenches.	
	10th "		In trenches.	
	11th "		Relieved by 8th Worcesters. Relief complete 9.30 p.m. Back to Bar Res. Colincamps. All in billets 10.30 p.m.	
Colincamps	12th "		Working parties; and baths at COLINCAMPS.	
	13th "		do.	
	14th "		do. Baths at SAILLY.	

WAR DIARY or INTELLIGENCE SUMMARY

Army Form C. 2118.

Place	Date	Hour	Summary of Events and Information	Remarks and references to Appendices
In trenches	July 15th		Relieved the 8th Worcesters in trenches. Relief complete about 6.45 p.m.	
59 R.B.H.	16		In trenches. Lieut S.E. Lloyd was killed by a rifle bullet when visiting Post 10 K.B.H. 6.9.2.	
	17		Lieut S.E. Lloyd buried with military honours at LOUVENCOURT. LEGEND shelled for considerable period with 5.9" shells.	H.Q.W.W.
	18		Considerable shelling especially of trench LEGEND by 5.9" shells.	
	19		At 2 a.m. enemy commenced shelling our own and the front line of the 6th Gloucesters on our left very heavily. Our support line was also shelled. I soon seemed evident that a cutting out expedition was intended. After about 30 minutes the fire on our own line lessened but increased in intensity on the Gloucesters. The Artillery covering us the 2nd Glos. Battery & West Riding Battery put up a magnificent barrage which probably prevented any Germans coming out of the trenches opposite U. Opposite the 6th Gloucesters about 200 of the enemy worked their way down a hedge and attacked the Gloucesters posts. The Gloucesters who had been heavily shelled with gas shells fought magnificently and although many of them suffered from gas and they had fairly heavy casualties they repulsed the enemy, took one prisoner and believe that they inflicted pretty severe losses on the enemy. The gas shells affected the eyes of our own men although no gas shells it is thought were fired into our sector. Our casualties were 5 men wounded. Relieved by 8th Worcesters at 9.30 p.m. Relief complete by 10.30 p.m. Total casualties for tour of duty in trenches 20.	

WAR DIARY
or
INTELLIGENCE SUMMARY.
(Erase heading not required.)

Summary of Events and Information	Remarks and references to Appendices

Capt Goodwin returns off leave.
Relieved 5th Glos in G Section of trenches 57 D.K.2.3. LT. MELHUISH and
1 N.C.O. report at Divisional School for course. Weather good.
Trenches drying well and weather magnificent. Conference by
G.O.C. Division of C.O.'s and Adjutants at 11-30 a.m. 6 men wounded.
Weather cooler but fine. G.O.C's Divisional conference 2-30 p.m.
on SAILLY SPUR.
Quiet day.
G.O.C. Division conference for C.O's and Adjutants and Staff on
SAILLY SPUR. at 9-0 p.m. Enemy bombards Brigade on our
right heavily till 10-30 p.m. Battalions stood to on alarm positions
Quiet.
Relieved in trenches by 8th Worcesters and proceeded to huts in
COVIN. "B" & "C" Coys Unends but together from SAILLY SPUR.
COVIN. Companies at disposal of O.C. Coys for cleaning up, etc.
Brigade Church parade in Chateau Grounds.

WAR DIARY
or
INTELLIGENCE SUMMARY.

Army Form C. 2118.

Place	Date	Hour	Summary of Events and Information	Remarks and references to Appendices
Billets	1916. April 1		Capt Goodwin returns off leave.	
	2.		Relieved 3rd Glos in "G" Section of trenches 57 D.K.23. LT. MELHUISH and 1 N.C.O. report at Divisional School for course. Weather good.	
Trenches.	3.		Trenches drying well and weather magnificent. Conference by G.O.C. Division of C.O's and Adjutants at 11-30 a.m. 6 men wounded.	
"	4.		Weather cooler but fine. G.O.C's Division conference 2-30 p.m. on SAILLY SPUR.	
"	5.		Quiet day.	
"	6.		G.O.C. Division conference for C.O's and Adjutants and Staff on SAILLY SPUR. at 9-0 p.m. Enemy bombarded Brigade on our right heavily till 10-30 p.m. Battalions stood to on alarm positions.	
"	7.		Quiet.	
"	8.		Relieved in trenches by 8th Worcesters and proceeded to huts in COUIN. "B" "C" Coys marched back together from SAILLY SPUR.	
Billets	9.		COUIN. Companies at disposal of O.C. Coys for cleaning up. etc. Brigade Church Parade in Chateau Grounds.	

Army Form C. 2118.

WAR DIARY
or
INTELLIGENCE SUMMARY.
(Erase heading not required.)

Instructions regarding War Diaries and Intelligence Summaries are contained in F. S. Regs., Part II. and the Staff Manual respectively. Title pages will be prepared in manuscript.

Place	Date	Hour	Summary of Events and Information	Remarks and references to Appendices
Billets.	April 1916. 10		COUIN. — Training	
"	11		"	
"	12		"	
"	13		"	
"	14		Relieved 8th Worcesters in E Section of Trenches at 11.30 p.m.	
Trenches.	15		The 145 Bde. Artillery bombarded for a few minutes enemy lines in front of this trench.	
"	16			#9(b)
"	17			
"	18			
"	19			
"	20			
"	21		Relieved in Trenches by BUCKS. Battalion and moved to Billets at BAYENCOURT, all but right & Centre Coy for trench platoons relieved in morning. Remainder back to Billets at 12.30 a.m.	

WAR DIARY
or
INTELLIGENCE SUMMARY.
(Erase heading not required.)

Army Form C. 2118.

Place	Date	Hour	Summary of Events and Information	Remarks and references to Appendices
	1916 April			
Bulls	22		BAYENCOURT. Cleaning up.	
"	23		Church parade 10.0 am in School of Instruction. Capt. Ashead returns off leave. "D" Coy commences firing musketry.	} #9104
"	24		"D" Coy continue to fire musketry. Remaining Coys drill etc. G.O.C. division holds conference for tactical exercises.	
"	25		Relieved Bucks Battalion in trenches. Relief complete 9.30 p.m. "D" right, "B" Coy centre, "C" left. "A" Reserve. West Yorks on our right. 4" Vl. Glos on our left.	
Trenches	26			
"	27			
"	28			
"	29		Lieut Reading killed in night fire trench by 5.9" shell at 11.30 p.m. Very intense bombardment on our right by 29th Division.	
"	30		4 men wounded.	

A. R. Harman
Comdg. 1/7th Bn. Worcestershire Regt.

Place	Date	Hour	Summary of Events and Information	Remarks and references to Appendices
BEAUVAL	1916 Thursday 9		Rules. Company Training. A wet day Route march cancelled	
	10		LT. COL. A.R. HARMAN resumed command of the Battalion. Inoculation "C" Coy. Inoculated	
	11		Inoculation "D" Coy. Inoculated. Bn issued with Short Rifles.	
	12		Transport inspection at 2:30 p.m. by Brigadier. Companies musketry training during morning.	
	13		Brigade Sports. 9th Worcesters won cup. 100 yards 9th Worcesters 1st 3 places. 1 Pte Bratley 2 Pte Antwell Hurdles :- 2/Lt. GORRIE. J.W. Lt. DIXON. J.E. Mile :- 1. Pte Clery 2. Pte Crew	

INTELLIGENCE SUMMARY.
(Erase heading not required.)

Summaries are contained in F. S. Regs., Part II.
and the Staff Manual respectively. Title pages
will be prepared in manuscript.

Place	Date	Hour	Summary of Events and Information	Remarks and references to Appendices
	1916			
BEAUVAL.	May 14		Brigade Parade Service. Distribution of Sports Prizes by Col. W.K. PEAKE	
	15		Brigade march from BEAUVAL. Bn billeted at COIGNEUX E 57 D 5 9 d 2 in tents and huts.	
COIGNEUX	16		Musketry. Working parties for 500 men.	
	17		At 6-0 p.m. the Bn paraded 580 strong and marched to "H" Cohn. Starting at 9-30 p.m. the Bn. dug a support line and 3 communication trenches to the "new trench" - 57 D. K.17.a.c. finishing the task [82 cub. ft per man] at 2-0 a.m.	
	18		Musketry training and baths.	
	19		Musketry training	
	20		Working parties for 500 men	
	21		Working parties. Reminder Church Parade 11-0 a.m.	
	22		Working parties. Scheme carried out in conjunction with R.O.C.	
	23.		Working parties.	

INTELLIGENCE SUMMARY.
(Erase heading not required.)

Place	Date	Hour	Summary of Events and Information	Remarks and references to Appendices
	1916 Aug 24		Relieved 8th Worcesters in G Section [57DK17 e.4.2 to K23d 2.4] relief complete 8-0 p.m. Quiet night.	
Trenches	25		4th Gloucestershire Regt on left - 16th York & Lancs Regt on our right. Trenches quiet day.	
	26		Brigadier visited trenches with new B.G.C. 113rd Inf Bde. Br Gen HOARE RUTHVEN G.S.O.1. VIII Corps also visited the Section	CRW
	27		Enemy appeared to be registering 1st Road Barricade and Prescott Ave with 5.9 Some shelling during night.	
	28		Company relief - enemy caused trouble on our cache with trench mortars and canister bombs. B Coy 1 Killed 3 Wounded during the night. Enemy shelling HEBUTERNE during the afternoon.	
	29		Quiet day. Enemy again sent over many canister bombs between 12 and 2 a.m. Sergt Snow killed. Our artillery retaliated. Nº 179 Sergt Snow Killed. Nº 2182 A/Cpl Hughes 'D' Coy killed by a small T.M. Bomb on the night during the afternoon 9.23 Shelled the point. Result appeared good.	

Army Form C. 2118.

1/7 Worcesters Regt

Vol 16

Min Bram (2)   M.16

WAR DIARY
or
INTELLIGENCE SUMMARY.
(Erase heading not required.)

Instructions regarding War Diaries and Intelligence Summaries are contained in F. S. Regs., Part II. and the Staff Manual respectively. Title pages will be prepared in manuscript.

Place	Date	Hour	Summary of Events and Information	Remarks and references to Appendices
	JUNE 1916			
TRENCHES 57D R.14.c R3d	1		Relieved by 4th Batt. the Royal Warwickshire Regiment. Relief complete 10.15 a.m. Bath marched to huts in CODIN PARK.	
GEZAINCOURT 57D. N.20.d	2		Batt. marched 5.0 a.m for march to the ST RIQUIER TRAINING AREA. Reached billets in GEZAINCOURT at 10.0 a.m.	
do	3		Resting. Baths for all the men.	
NEUVILLE	4		Paraded 7.0 a.m to continue march. Breakfast en route near BERNATRE. All in billets at NEUVILLE by 12.45 p.m.	
do	5		Manoeuvre Exercises. Training area appeared to be very suitable.	
do	6		do. Heavy rain.	
do	7		do. Again very heavy rain.	
do	8		do. Divisional scheme with 145th Infantry Brigade.	
do	9		do. Weather not improved.	
do	10		do. Divisional Scheme.	
do	11		do	
do	12		Batt. paraded for a Scheme, which was cancelled owing to heavy rain. Marched to billets in YVRENCHEUX [2½ miles]. Billets not good. Men wet.	

Army Form C. 2118.

WAR DIARY
or
INTELLIGENCE SUMMARY.
(Erase heading not required.)

Instructions regarding War Diaries and Intelligence Summaries are contained in F. S. Regs., Part II. and the Staff Manual respectively. Title pages will be prepared in manuscript.

Place	Date	Hour	Summary of Events and Information	Remarks and references to Appendices
	JUNE 1916.			
VARENNEUX.	12 (cont)		In this evening party of "B" Coy. [Officers Capts H. W. ADSHEAD, H. & W. WOOD, Lieuts J.G. DIXON and J.W. H. MELHUISH] left for SAILLY to re-traverse raid on enemy trenches.	
do	13.		Homeworks Exercises	
do	14.		Prepared for a day of rest, prior to a hastened return Eastwards. On 15th at 12.30 p.m. orders received to march at 2.0 p.m. Marched over bad roads to good billets in NEZEROLLES. [6 miles W of DOULLENS] arrived 7.30 p.m. Men lost an hours rest due to Daylight Saving Scheme.	
NEZEROLLES	15.		Bath paraded 4.0 a.m. to continue march. Breakfasts en route near DOULLENS. Marched past Corps Commander and G.O.C. Division at AUTHIE all in camp at LOIGNEUX [57D.V9d] at 1.0 p.m. Every man came in with Batln having marched 30 miles in 28 hours. "B" Coy attempted raid on enemy trenches at night failed through bad luck. Sappers of 3rd S.M. Fld. Coy R.E. co-operating with them behaved very gallantly.	See copy of report attached.
COIGNEUX	16		Working parties. 100 O.R.	
do	17		do 350 O.R.	
do	18		do 500 O.R.	

1577 Wt. W10791/1773 500,000 1/15 D. D. & L. A.D.S.S./Forms/C. 2118.

Army Form C. 2118.

WAR DIARY
or
INTELLIGENCE SUMMARY.
(Erase heading not required.)

Place	Date	Hour	Summary of Events and Information	Remarks and references to Appendices
COIGNEUX	JUNE 1916			
	19		Working parties. 590 O.R. 200 men carrying 180 LBS French Mortar Ammunition.	
	20		do 200 O.R. All this working parties found by the Battr during this	
			period were for tasks directly connected with preparations for an advance.	
	21		Working parties. 450 officers and men formed part of a gang under Major F.	
			M. Tomkinson carrying gas cylinders to prepared positions on the front line.	
	22		Working parties. 560 O.R. 2Lieut L.J. WAREHAM joined from the Base.	
	23		do 400 O.R. Lieut K.C. BAXTER and 63 O.R. went to AUTHIEULE	
			as a detached working party.	
	24		1st Day of Bombardment ["U" day] Companies training and experimenting	
			as to the best method of carrying all the equipment necessary for the attack.	
	25		"V" day. Heavy thunderstorm in the afternoon. Companies training	
	26		"W" day. More rain. Companies training. 2Lieut J.C. HUMPHRIES rejoined Battn.	
	27		"X" day. Final arrangements being made. Still raining.	
	28		"Y" day. The assault arranged for 28th is postponed for 48 hours. Ground very wet	
			"B" Coy [75 O.R and Capts. H.W. ADSHEAD. H.G.W. WOOD. 2Lieuts J.G. DIXON and	
			J.D.W. METHUISH] attempted a raid on enemy trenches. The raid failed	Report attached

Army Form C. 2118.

WAR DIARY
or
INTELLIGENCE SUMMARY.
(Erase heading not required.)

Instructions regarding War Diaries and Intelligence Summaries are contained in F. S. Regs., Part II. and the Staff Manual respectively. Title pages will be prepared in manuscript.

Place	Date	Hour	Summary of Events and Information	Remarks and references to Appendices
POIGNEUX	JUNE 1916			
	28. (con)		owing to lack of time for reconnaissance and preparation.	
	29.		2 day. Bombardment continues. Very cloudy but rain held off. Companies training	
	30.		Bombardment continues.	
			Total Casualties for 15 months ending 30th June 1916.	
			Killed - Officers 3 Other Ranks 20	
			Wounded - " 7 " 179	
			Died of Wounds " 1 " 10	
			Died of Sickness " 2 " 5	
			A. R. Harman Lieut. Col.	
			commdg 4th Batln The Worcestershire Regiment.	

CONFIDENTIAL.

WAR DIARY,

OF

7th WORCESTERSHIRE REGIMENT.

FROM 1st JULY, 1916 to 31st JULY, 1916.

(VOL: JULY, 1916.)

WAR DIARY or INTELLIGENCE SUMMARY

Army Form C.2118.

Place	Date	Hour	Summary of Events and Information	Remarks and references to Appendices
COIGNEUX	1916 July 1	12·50 a.m.	Recd. O.O. No 62 - 6·30 a.m. recd. Bn. O.O. No.1. 7·30 a.m. Recd. O.O. 63.	
		7·45 a.m.	Recd Message from Corps Commander. 8·0 a.m. Bn. parade to rendezvous at J.15.c.6.3, 8·75 a.m. Recd. Zero time for march table as 8·0 a.m. this orders were received at 8·15 a.m. to pass the starting point at 8·22 a.m. !!!	
		9·30 a.m.	Recd message from Army Commander	
J.15.c.5.3		9·30 a.m.	Bttn. marched via BERTRANCOURT - BEAUSSART to J.18.C. S.W. of MAILLY MAILLET	
" J.18.c		11·10 a.m.	Bttn. arrived 11·10 a.m.	
"		12 noon	Recd orders to store packs & greatcoats in the event of a forward move	
"		12·50 p.m.	Recd. instructions that the Bttn could halt for several hours.	
"		6·12 p.m.	C.O's conference at Bde. - no news	
"		7·40 a.m.	Recd. General Summary [XIII] & XV Corps & French doing well - 5,700 prisoners	
	2		Some guns captured] 9·0 a.m. C.O's conference at Bde. [VIII] Corps now Fifth Army. - all VIII Corps troops had been withdrawn to our original front line. Defensive flank not at SERRE but to be formed Y RAVINE - STATION ROAD - High ground S of ANCRE - This to be done by H"Kin"n preliminary orders for the attack.	
"		10·0 a.m.	C.O. went with B.G.C. to make reconnaissance. 12·70 a.m. Recd orders to get the Battalion under cover in the shrub.	

WAR DIARY
or
INTELLIGENCE SUMMARY.
(Erase heading not required.)

Army Form C. 2118.

Instructions regarding War Diaries and Intelligence Summaries are contained in F. S. Regs., Part II. and the Staff Manual respectively. Title pages will be prepared in manuscript.

Place	Date	Hour	Summary of Events and Information	Remarks and references to Appendices
J.18.C.	2.	5-0 p.m.	issued Bn. O.O. No.2. 6-15 p.m Read O.O. No 64.(?)	
		7-45 p.m.	Bn. paraded less officers & men detailed for 1st reinforcement, strength 690 all ranks. 8-0 p.m. marched from Bus starting point via ENGLEBELMER to approx	
Q.20.6		10 p.m	Q 20 b where after half 6th Glos moved forward via GABION AV and Bn. via WITHINGTON AV.	
Q.22.6		11.15 p.m.	Converged with 6th Glos at KNIGHTSBRIDGE owing to non-existent or totally inadequate traffic control. Neither Bn. could advance owing to odd ration parties & wounded men coming back. 6th Glos eventually started & after 10 mins were further blocked by a Company of Essex Regt. returning from front line. 6th Glos just clearing our front at 12-30 p.m.	
"		12-20 a.m.	Heard verbal message being passed up 6th Glos line - "Meet in front from the Brigadier" - Fact, all operations cancelled. 6th Glos turned about & began to return	
"	3rd	12-30 a.m	Recd. S.C.O 2 All operations for to-night cancelled. Return to bivouacs MAILLY MAILLET about.	
"		12.40 a.m	Began to return by same route as we had come. Progress very slow men two deep in the trench - 4th Glos & 4th Monmouths in trench trying to come in opposite direction. Progress further impeded by constant passing of unauthentic and contradictory messages. Bn. finally dribbled out of the end of the trench at about 3-45 a.m. Platoons	

Army Form C. 2118.

WAR DIARY
or
INTELLIGENCE SUMMARY.
(Erase heading not required.)

Place	Date	Hour	Summary of Events and Information	Remarks and references to Appendices
	July 1916			
J.18.C.	4	3-30 pm	Marched back to J.18.C independently all in about 11-0 a.m. 1 man wounded, 1 man 'A' Coy Missing. Recd B.M.O. of "The Bn. will march to Bivouac at COUIN or COIGNEUX at 5.0 pm this afternoon	
"		3-50 "	Issued Bn. O.O. No 3. 4-25 pm Recd. O.O. No 65. 4-50 pm Bn. marched via BEAUSSART — BERTRANCOURT — J.15.C.5.3. thence to original positions — Bn. to camp at COIGNEUX — very trying march conditions.	
COIGNEUX	5	10-10 pm	Recd. B.M. 2. Bn at 2 hours notice	
"	6.	9-30 am	Recd. B.M. 5. Stand down. Bn rested during the day.	
"	7		Working Parties 250. O.R.	
"	8		Working Parties & baths.	
			Relieved 8th Worcs in the trenches & cleaned occupied 57 D. K.29.C.89 to K.35 a.6.9. Trenches very battered and full of debris and dead. 4th Glos on left, 1st S.L.I on right.	
	9th 10th 11th 12th		In trenches — much salvage and cleaning work. Weather on the whole good.	
COIGNEUX	13	5-0 pm	Relieved by 8th Worcs. — Relief complete by 5-45 pm. Bn. back to camp at COIGNEUX C.O. to Bde Conference at COURCELLES heard that H.Q. Bde were to demonstrate to assist further attack by Fourth Army. Heard casually from G.O.C. Division	

Army Form C. 2118.

WAR DIARY
or
INTELLIGENCE SUMMARY.
(Erase heading not required.)

Instructions regarding War Diaries and Intelligence Summaries are contained in F. S. Regs., Part II. and the Staff Manual respectively. Title pages will be prepared in manuscript.

Place	Date	Hour	Summary of Events and Information	Remarks and references to Appendices
COIGNEUX	14	9.30 p.m	that this Bde was moving S. almost at once.	
		9.30 p.m	Recd. G.R. 518 Bde being relieved by 115th Bde 38' Div to-morrow.	
"		9.30 am.	Recd S.O. 163 "Be ready to move at a moments notice.	
"		10-0 am	Asked Bde. if verbal orders of 13th re marching out in fighting order held good.	
"		10-15 am	Recd B.M. 86 saying busses will arrive about 1-0 p.m. to move you. recd Bulletin of Army.	
"		10-45 am	Recd instructions to march out in full marching order. Verbal orders of 13th having already been acted upon. many packs had to be fetched out of store again.	
"		1-20 p.m	Recd D.O. no 70. Camp handed over to 6th R. Welsh Regt.	
"		3-10 p.m	Bn. paraded dinners up into parties of 1 Officer & 22 OR. for entraining purposes	
"		3-0 p.m	Busses arrived 3-40 p.m. all on board. Started via BERTRANCOURT – FORCEVILLE – HEDAUVILLE – BOUZINCOURT.	
BOUZINCOURT	15	5-30 p.m	Adjutant & Major F.M.T. to find Town Major & billets found billets in huts N. of village [approx 57D. W8.c.1.8] Bn. in billets 6-45 p.m. 9-0 p.m Transport & Bn. all in.	
"		8.0 am	Received O.O. no. 70. 1/2. 10.0 am C.O. & OR. at Bde this Bde relieves 14th Bde. 32nd Div. to-night. C.O. O.O.C. Coys to make reconnaissance.	
"		5-0 p.m	Head of Bn. moved out to commence relief fighting order. A & B Companies	

WAR DIARY
or
INTELLIGENCE SUMMARY
Army Form C. 2118.

Place	Date	Hour	Summary of Events and Information	Remarks and references to Appendices
	15th (cont)		to relieve 761 Dorsets. C.O. to relieve 2nd Manchesters - Relief complete 10.30 pm Situation in front line [57D] on our right 75th Inf Bde holding line X.8.b.3.1. to X.8.a.9.2. thence our Battalion X.8.b.3.1. to X.8.a.9.1. this point being in the neighbourhood alleged to have been the site of the church, thence through the village to point X.8.a.5.1 thence to a point in old German front line approx X.8.a.1.1.	CMW
X.6.c.3.3.		11.45 pm	Recd. Wire 99. Attack on Ovillers to be resumed Bn to Co-operate with 75th Inf Bde.	
		12.30 am	Issued B.W.1. B Coy to pivot on their left A Coy to keep touch with 75th Bde on our right.	
	16	2.0 am	We held 92 and 82 [A.H.4 to Bde.] no touch with 75th Bde. Enemy seen holding line 13-45. 3.0 a.m. A Coy in touch with 75th Bde. in their original position.	
		3.30 am	75th Bde not advancing their attacking Coy has been withdrawn reported to be waiting for 74th Bde. 4.30 am. The Bn. shot down. A.H.12 situation report to Bde " Present line X.8.a.05.09 to junction of road X.8.a.4.3. to 52 thence across to 72 to 62 to 92 to X.8.b.01 thence to 31. During day heavy shelling especially on own left Coy	

WAR DIARY
or
INTELLIGENCE SUMMARY.
(Erase heading not required.)

Army Form C. 2118.

Place	Date	Hour	Summary of Events and Information	Remarks and references to Appendices
X.9.c.3.3.		5.30 pm	Recd O.O. no 94. Bn to extend its front from 31 to 53 exclusive. Issued A.H. 13. "A" Coy to take over new front - and re-adjustments of Coy fronts.	
		6.10 pm	Recd B.M. 8.1. H.Glos attacking German front line X8a 05.20 to X7.b.99. Bn to co-operate by bombing from our left and an attempt to gain village.	
X.8.c.3.3.		7.45 pm	A.H. 17 to Bde "almost impossible to co-operate except on extreme left until Coys have taken over new dispositions. I propose using Flame Projector [Lieut ASTLEY R.E] on X8a 05.20 also co-operating on this section with Stokes Mortars M.G fire hoping to attain 2 results (1) to mark for H. Glos the left of their objective (2) to create a diversion"	
		8.55 pm	B.M. 134 "Glos attack will not take place unless patrols can find gaps in the wire" A.H. 19 & 21 giving orders to Coys etc in the event of an attack.	
		9.45 pm	Recd B.M.O 137. 170 Germans reported surrendered in OVILLERS press success E + N..."	
		9.50 pm	A.H. 22 to Bde "Write do what I can but relief of 75th Bde not yet commenced as they have no orders to hand over, also my line is very extended"	
		10.10 pm	Recd B.M.O. 138 7th Bde report enemy evacuating OVILLERS push on."	
		10.17 pm	A.H. 23 to all Coys "Push out small patrols & make good any ground	

WAR DIARY
or
INTELLIGENCE SUMMARY.

Army Form C. 2118.

Place	Date	Hour	Summary of Events and Information	Remarks and references to Appendices
X.8.C.33.			evacuated by enemy. 11=45 pm A.H 24. 25. 36.37 giving orders to Coys.	
			1st Objective 20-52- 63- 95 -16 after that Coys to bomb down communication trenches.	
		12 midnight	2nd "C" Coy first Lumphries patrol reached within 25 yds of trench 13-45 & was then opened on by M.G. also strong party tried to cut him off.	
			2nd B Coy Patrol moving out from CRATER report enemy holding line 63-95 with M.G.	
			[Casualties for the day 3 killed - 4 Wounded]	
	17	12-1 am	A.H 38 to B.H.C giving above intelligence another patrol is also working towards 16 & 74 Am not in touch with 143 Bde	
		12-14 am	A.H 39 to A Coy "You must get in touch with Warwicks at 53."	
		12-27 am	2nd "A" Coy "Have point 34, am pushing on to 16.	
		12-37 am	Rec'd B.M.O. 143 "Glos will commence their attack 2-0 am	
		12-32 am	A.H 30 to "A" Coy "Hang on to pt. 34 & wait for Warwicks there"	
		1-45 am	A.H 32 to "C" in the event of success of Glos attack sup(p)tng A.H 27 you will act as support to "B" Coy.	
		2-46 am	2nd "D" Coy "In touch with S Lancs at X 8.b.31 aweft 8th Barrier at X 8 C 83. Relief of 75th Bde by Warwicks in progress	

Army Form C. 2118.

WAR DIARY
or
INTELLIGENCE SUMMARY.
(Erase heading not required.)

Instructions regarding War Diaries and Intelligence Summaries are contained in F. S. Regs., Part II. and the Staff Manual respectively. Title pages will be prepared in manuscript.

Place	Date	Hour	Summary of Events and Information	Remarks and references to Appendices
X.8.c.3.3.		3.31 a.m.	Report from O.C. "C" Coy. that there are no signs of 4 Glos. in enemy trench	
		3.35 a.m.	H.W.A.3 from "B" Coy. "further advance towards 63-95 proves that this line is strongly held.	
		4.0 a.m.	From O.C. "A" Coy. "Present line 60 yds short of 16-44-53 [Listening post towards 56]. Trench 56-66 unoccupied. Warwicks could join up with me here but there are no signs of them. The line 63-95 is strongly held. There are three M.Gs	
		4-20 a.m.	R.M.O. 147 Glos report they were in enemy trench 2-30 a.m."	
		4.50 a.m.	A.H. 38 to Bde "We are not in touch with 4 Glos along old German front line" 16-95-63 seems to be strongly held	
		5-20 a.m.	From "B" Coy "We are still in touch with 'A' at the Church". Situation reports to Bde at 7.9.11. remained unchanged. No touch with 4 Glos. At 1.0 p.m. 4th Gloster bombing party up German old front line effected junction with 4 Glos advancing party of the previous night at about 1-30 p.m.	
		1-45 p.m.	received B.M.O. 161 objective required X.2.C.7.1.	
		3-30 p.m.	"A" Coy in touch with Warwicks at S.H. Issued Bn O.O. Zero time 4-30 /a.m. 1st Objective 45-63-95-16	

WAR DIARY
or
INTELLIGENCE SUMMARY.
(Erase heading not required.)

Army Form C. 2118.

Place	Date	Hour	Summary of Events and Information	Remarks and references to Appendices
Point 09	17th (contd)	5.30 p.m.	1st Objective made good – about 60 wounded prisoners reported at 16. Bn. HQrs. Moved to Point 09	
		5.45 p.m.	A.H. H.H. to all Coys giving orders for further advance to line 46-88-98.	
		6.45 p.m.	Recd. B.M.O. 175 "Do not advance further until written instructions reach you"	
		7.5 p.m.	A.H. 115 to Bdo. "Advance on line 46-88-95 has begun before receipt of your B.M.O. 175". This line is now made good. (Casualties for the day 1 Killed – 22 Wounded) at ABBEELE WOOD	
	18th	7.15 a.m.	Recd B.M.O. 177.	
		7.40 p.m.	A.H. H.7. H.8. H.9. to Coys giving orders for further advance to 71. 92. 02. 44 at 8.30 p.m.	
		10.0 p.m.	A.H. 54. to Bde "My present line is 71.92.02.44 thence down 44-78 to a point about X.2 & 53". R.E. & Sussex sent up to consolidate. Working remainder of night. D. Coy did good work carrying up rations, water, S.A.A. and bombs. No touch except at 46 with Glos.	
		1.0 p.m.	Recd. congratulations from Army Commander	
		1.15 p.m.	Recd. O.O. no 74. Further advance to be made by bombing parties to line 36-45 and further to 38-47".	

Army Form C. 2118.

WAR DIARY
or
INTELLIGENCE SUMMARY.
(Erase heading not required.)

Place	Date	Hour	Summary of Events and Information	Remarks and references to Appendices
Point 89	18th (cont)	1.30 pm	A.H. 61 to A.1.B. giving necessary orders.	
		5.0 pm	17 H. 63 to Bde. "28 & 47 made good enemy encountered in 28-88 are Glosters at 88.	
		6.0 pm	From H. Glos. "We are advancing as fast as we can - Ground very unfavourable.	
		7.10 pm	B.M.10 202 "Take over HH to 78 from 143 Bde."	
		7.15 pm	A.H. 66 to "A" giving instructions	
		8.30 pm	Enemy bombed our first out of 78 which was quite in the air	
		10.56 pm	H. Glos. established on line 37-66	
		11.0 pm	Various messages from O.C. B & H.A 42, 47, 49. making it clear that 2/Lt. CLARKE at 38 was forced to retire owing to his position being entirely unsupported on the flank.	
		11.0 pm	Enemy shelling heavily on line 92-03-44.	
		11.5 pm	Recd. O.O. No.75. Bn. C were points 90-62-03. Zero time 1-30 am	
		11.40 pm	A.H 69 to all Coys A to attack on the right B on the left C in support D in reserve	
		11.50 pm	O.C "B" Coy reports [H.A 50] that his front platoon very shaken by shell fire.	
		12 midnight	Bn. HQrs moved to Aug-out just N of 85.	
Point 85	19th	1.55 am	A.H. 71, 72, to A.1B. If M.G. fire too heavy fall back to original line	

1577 Wt.W.10791/1773 500,000 1/15 D.D.& L. A.D.S.S./Forms/C. 2118.

WAR DIARY
or
INTELLIGENCE SUMMARY.
(Erase heading not required.)

Army Form C.2118.

Place	Date	Hour	Summary of Events and Information	Remarks and references to Appendices
Form 85		2-3 a.m	Leaving slope at 38 & 36.	
			From O.C. 'A' Coy [A.B.17] "Send up to outpost me." 1 Platoon sent to O.C 'A' Coy at 3-5 a.m.	
		2-9 a.m.	A.H. 73 to 'C' When B falls back hold line from W.9 92. to 10."	
		2-11 a.m	A.H 74 to Bde. "Unable to advance owing to cross fire M.G."	
		2.55 a.m	From O.C. 'B' Coy "Reports held up at 38 3·5 a.m."	
		2-27 a.m	A.H. 75 to B. If you are held up by M.G. fall back through 'C' Coy in original line to line 86 – 46. A.H. 76 to Bde giving situation.	
		3.41 a.m	A.H. 77 G.B.	
		3-0 a.	From 'C' Coy B are retiring through us am holding 71-92-02. ¾	
		3-15 a.m	A.H. 78 to Bde giving final situation "grind but unable to hold enemy trench 62 near two Lewis Gun teams got into action but were lost. Left Coy for point 20 but were there held up by M.G. fire + enemy counter-attacked. Am now holding original line.	
			Final situation D ✓ C holding original line. A + B re-organising in trench 16 – 95 – 63.	
		5-40 a.m	H.Q. Bde report they are holding 88 & patrolling towards 38. A.H. 84 reply	

WAR DIARY
or
INTELLIGENCE SUMMARY.

Army Form C. 2118.

Place	Date	Hour	Summary of Events and Information	Remarks and references to Appendices
Point 85			that we are not in touch with them. Further at 6.30am C. report having visited 88 & found signs of a recent fight. O.O. aim. we withdraw to 36. Situation remains unchanged during the remainder of the day & night. 19/30 . Heavy enemy shelling. Casualties for 2 days 18/19" 36 killed – 2/Lt CORRIE + 2/Lt GOUGH. 120 Wounded	
	20.	10.30a	C.O. heard we are to be relieved by 8th Wore. Relief orders issued.	
		2.10p	Reed B.M.O. 287 Relief cancelled.	
		4.30pm	Reed O.O. No 17 attack to be continued. An objective 90 — to X 3 a 2 3 zero time 2–45 a.m – 6th Glosc to attack on our right (Left), 145 Bde on our right	
		6.45pm	A.H. 89 B to attack A to relieve D at once. Casualties for the day 2 Wounded.	
	21.	2.47am	From O.C. "D" Coy deployed at 1–35 am	
		3.30am	Heard through A Coy that D were in enemy trench. Sent up Pioneer Platoon (5th Royal Sussex) to dig 36–47 and 45–47	
		3.50am	From O.C. D showing present position in trench leading towards 90 from just North of 44–47 trying to bomb to 90. Glos cannot get forward for M.G.F. A.H. 93 to Bde. giving situation.	
		4.30am	From A that D are relieving Sussex also return. A.H. 95 to Bde	

WAR DIARY
or
INTELLIGENCE SUMMARY.
(Erase heading not required.)

Army Form C. 2118.

Place	Date	Hour	Summary of Events and Information	Remarks and references to Appendices
		4.30 a.m.	CAPT ADAM came to Bn. HQrs. He reached dummy trench in front of Objective but deep mud prevented an advance by bombing in either direction. Blos being badly held up on his left. CAPT ADAM covered their retirements then fell back himself, his position being untenable in daylight.	
		6.5 a.m.	Received B.M.O. 360 Right Bde arranging further attack	
		6.30 a.m.	Letter from B.G.C. Relief to take place today. Also received B.M.O. 264 to same effect.	
			The Bn. who were not relieved by 8th Worc. but A.2.C. were relieved by 6th Glos. who then took on the Bde. front line. These Companies went to shelters in RIBBLE STREET. B & D Coys were withdrawn to dug-outs at CRUCIFIX CORNER. Cookers came up. Also relief of officers from BOUZINCOURT. Casualties for the day 2 killed 2/Lts WAREHAM & BROWNFAIN 14 O.R. wounded 2 missing. Bn. reaching Coys available for interior economy.	
22		4.0 p.m	Received O.O. 79 Bde to continue advance. 6th Glouc to attack night of 22/90. Bn. to remain in a position of readiness about RIBBLE ST. approx 3.0 a.m.	
23		2.0 a.m	Bn. position 1.0 a.m hill 3.30 km Bn. back in quarters about 4.0 a.m. Recd O.O. no 81 to relieve 4th Glouc.	

1577 Wt.W10791/1773 500,000 1/15 D.D./L. A.D.S.S./Forms/C. 2118.

Army Form C. 2118.

WAR DIARY
or
INTELLIGENCE SUMMARY.

(Erase heading not required.)

Instructions regarding War Diaries and Intelligence Summaries are contained in F. S. Regs., Part II. and the Staff Manual respectively. Title pages will be prepared in manuscript.

Place	Date	Hour	Summary of Events and Information	Remarks and references to Appendices
	24.		Relieved H'Glouse in the trenches. Relief complete 11-0 a.m. E.O.C. visited trenches during the afternoon.	
	25	1-4 a.m.	Bttn on our right [145] attacked. Bn demonstrated to locate enemy. Bn were heavily shelled during night by 5-9 hour: Advanced posts shewn to contact aeroplanes by means of flares. Hostile artillery activity very active especially Bn. HQrs at which a heavy gun fires every ten minutes.	
	26		Recd O.O. No.83 Bn to be relieved by 6th Bn. Queens Own R.W. Kent Regt. POZIERES heavily shelled in the morning. E.O.C. round from line – things seemed quieter on the whole.	
	27		Bn relieved by 6th Q.O.R.W.K. 1-0 p.m. Bn to HEDAUVILLE arriving en route Bn all in Billets by 5-0 p.m.	
	28		Bttn to ARQUEVES. Bn paraded 7-5 a.m. all in billets 10-30 a.m.	
	29		Bttn to BEAUVAL. Bn parade 7-35 a.m. all in billets 11-0 a.m. Bn occupied same billets as in May of this year.	
	30.		Bttn to DOMART area. Bn parade 10-5 a.m. marched to surcamps breakfast. En route near FIENVILLERS. all in billets 12 noon. Only 3 men out.	

Army Form C. 2118.

WAR DIARY
or
INTELLIGENCE SUMMARY.
(Erase heading not required.)

Instructions regarding War Diaries and Intelligence Summaries are contained in F. S. Regs., Part II. and the Staff Manual respectively. Title pages will be prepared in manuscript.

Place	Date	Hour	Summary of Events and Information	Remarks and references to Appendices
	31		Area totally inadequate to provide accommodation. Men all in Orchards. Water supply very short. Bn. resting. Message received from G.O.C. 11 Corps.	

R. Harman Lieut. Col.
Comdg. 1/7th Bn. Worcestershire Regt.

INTELLIGENCE SUMMARY

(Erase heading not required.)

Place	Date	Hour	Summary of Events and Information	Remarks and references to Appendices
SURCAMPS	August 1916 1		Company training. Water supply very uncertain.	
	2		do. Companies marched to pools at L'ETOILE to bathe in the evening.	
	3		C.O. inspected "A" & "B" Companies	
	4		do. "C" & "D" Cinema show in the evening.	
	5		Companies training. R.Cos on pass to ABBEVILLE	
	6		Sunday Church Parade 11-0 a.m.	
	7		Bn. inspected by Brigadier	
	8		Companies training.	
CANDAS	9		Bn. move trinked 6-30 a.m. to CANDAS all in 10-30 a.m.	
PUCHVILLERS	10		Bn. marched via cross country track which gave certain difficulty to the Transport to PUCHVILLERS; all in 12 noon. About 1 mile from home H.M. The KING motored part the Bn on the march.	
	11		Will not move to-day	
FORCEVILLE	12		Bn. marched to FORCEVILLE; all in 11-15 a.m. LT. A.D LLOYD and 68 O.R from Base Depot	
W.F.d.	13		Sunday Church Parade 11-0 a.m. Bn marched 2-0 p.m to bivouacs 57 D W 8 d. 4+6 Kilometers took over line from 37th Inf Bde.	

INTELLIGENCE SUMMARY

(Erase heading not required.)

Place	Date	Hour	Summary of Events and Information	Remarks and references to Appendices
AUGUST 1916				
X2 a 8.5	21 (cont?)	2.24 p.m.	From LT. PEAKE via O.C. 'D' situation between 76-79 apparently unchanged.	
		2.30 p.m.	Report from O.C. 'D' that 76-79 not enough to allow communication.	
		3-5 p.m.	From O.C. 'B' to communication with 110yds. 4-5 p.m. From O.C. 'D' sent 1 platoon to attack 91 with LT HILL. Failed to reach objective. Situation 76-79 unchanged. 4.32 p.m. From O.C. 'D' giving dispositions. LIEUT. HILL has returned. 4.40 p.m. A.H. 58 'C' to relieve 'D'. 4-50 p.m. A.H. 60 to 'B' & 'C' offensive to cease consolidate. 8.15 p.m. From O.C. 'C' Enemy made bombing attack from 79 against our stop there at 7.30 p.m. she was driven off. Enta. at 6.0 p.m. 4" Glos. made an attack on enemy on original front line in X.1.a.2.b. This was unsuccessful and at 9.45 p.m. 6" Glos. reported touch with 4" Glos at 81. 9.115 p.m. A.H. 63 to O.C. 'C' "6" Glos report touch with 4" Glos at 81. 6" Glos now trying to bomb to 79 from 27, you must bomb to 79."	
	22	2-6 a.m.	From O.C. 'C' Have made several attacks on 79. No success. 3-30 a.m. A.H. 69 to O.C. 'C' without further attacks and prepare for organised effort in daylight. 5.40 a.m. Enemy reported to have re-taken 31 wearing British uniform. 6.10 a.m. Situation on our left obscure - apparently 6" Glos held 19-26 and stop between 16 and 117. Enemy at 81 between 6" & 4" Glos. 8.45 a.m. R.H. 75 to O.C. 'C' Have everything in readiness to attack 79 (see A.H. 69 above). 9-45 a.m. from 6 Glos. Situation, we are about 50x S. of 19. We held 27 and trench junction between 27 and 29. 11-30 a.m. A.H. 76 to O.C 'B' "Hand over 59 to 8 R.W.R. 12-30 p.m. A.H. 77 to O.C 6 Glos acting when he will be ready to move forward again. 3-40 p.m. Recd OO No 102 4"& 6" Glos. to attack 81 at 12=0 p.m.	

INTELLIGENCE SUMMARY

(Erase heading not required.)

Place	Date	Hour	Summary of Events and Information	Remarks and references to Appendices
			Casualties for month of August 1916	
			Killed Wounded Officers	
			Total 33 123 3 Wounded	
			20th 19 25 1 do	
			21st 8 43 1 do	
			22nd 2 41 1 do	
			61 142	

A. R. Holman
Comdg. 1/7th Bn. Worcestershire Regt.

Army Form C. 2118.

1/7 Worcester Regt

WAR DIARY
or
INTELLIGENCE SUMMARY

(Erase heading not required.)

Vol 19

Place	Date	Hour	Summary of Events and Information	Remarks and references to Appendices
B.A.W.93 37D	September 1916 1		Weather fine, occasional shelling, two guns were cutting	
	2		Weather fine. "B" Coy in AUCHONVILLERS	
	3		Y Coys (39 & 49 "Kins) attack on our right - attack failed.	
	4		More rain. Bus left off successfully about 6.30 p.m. Short relaxation.	
BUS-LES-	5		Bn. moved to BUS, going from MAILLY in motor buses. Relieved by 1/1st Oxford & Bucks	
ARTOIS	6		Relief complete 11.0 a.m. In huts near Colincamps	
	7		Company training. Companies training - training in early morning - bombing and musketry. Officers joined the Bn. 2/Lts BROWN W.N.S., LEAKE R.S., GADSBY F.L., and NESS H.N.E.	
	8		Bn. inspected by MAJOR-GEN R. FANSHAWE D.S.O. C.B. Military Medals were presented at this parade to 3167 Corpl Cope S., 1658 Yct Barlow J., 1884 Pte Buick J., 1927 Pte Drew A.B., 1891 Pte Wassell having been wounded could not receive their medals. Bayonet fighting course begun.	
	9		Battalion parade - A.C. Coys rode to SARTON (butts)	
	10.		Church Parade outside CHATEAU. D.C.M. awarded to 2469 Pte Roper S.	
	11		D.S.O. awarded to LIEUT. J.C.M. HILL. Conference practising advanced guards. Working party of 250 - filling in cable trench near BERTRANCOURT. "C" Coy on the range	11.19
AMPLIER	12.		Battalion moved to AMPLIER, on the way commence in ordering formations in conjunction with 6th Glos. Rain began as Bn. entered new Billets.	
	13.		Coys practising advance guards, feint and rear guards. Military medal awarded to 3973 Pte Havens J., 1447 Pte Cotton McDighe J.	
	14			

2449 Wt. W14957/M90 750,000 1/16 J.B.C. & A. Forms/C.2118/12.

Army Form C. 2118.

WAR DIARY
or
INTELLIGENCE SUMMARY
(Erase heading not required.)

Instructions regarding War Diaries and Intelligence Summaries are contained in F. S. Regs., Part II. and the Staff Manual respectively. Title Pages will be prepared in manuscript.

Place	Date	Hour	Summary of Events and Information	Remarks and references to Appendices
September 1916				
AMPLIER	15		Bathing. Company training, musketry & elementary outpost scheme.	
	16		Company training - outposts - musketry & extended order	
	17		Divine Service. Lecture on bayonet fighting by Capt HUNTINGTON. 2529 Pte H. Tibbetts awarded the Cross of St George. (1st Class)	
LE MEILLARD	18		Bn. moved to LE MEILLARD. Weather rather wet and blustery. Everyone soaked on arrival.	
	19		Training. C.O.'s parade. Special message of congratulations from H.M. THE KING. Leave parties began.	
	20		Coys training	
	21		Coys training. The Company in attack	
	22		Coys bathing at BERNAVILLE. Conference at Bde HQRS at 3-0 p.m. D.S.O awarded to LT.COL A.R HARMAN	
	23		Bn. practised an attack.	
	24		Voluntary Church Parade. The Rifle Commander's Snap Shooting Competition held at BOISBERGUES. 2 Officers & 23 other ranks proceed to rest camp at AULT. Bde conference at AUTHEUX	
	25		Bn practises attack with "B" "C" Coys. A.T.D. Bathing at BERNAVILLE. Weather very fine.	
	26		Coys training, musketry extended order bayonet fighting.	
	27		Coys training. Rapid practices on range. Divisional Staff rode 30 km	

Army Form C. 2118.

WAR DIARY
or
INTELLIGENCE SUMMARY
(Erase heading not required.)

Instructions regarding War Diaries and Intelligence Summaries are contained in F.S. Regs., Part II. and the Staff Manual respectively. Title Pages will be prepared in manuscript.

Place	Date 1916	Hour	Summary of Events and Information	Remarks and references to Appendices
LE MEILLARD	September 28		Divisional Tactical Scheme – route march and attack on MT RENAULT FM. RIDGE ending with attack on BERNAVILLE.	
	29		Very Wet. Bde Tactical scheme cancelled. Coy.s at disposal of Coy commanders. Lecture on Sanitation.	
IVERGNY	30		Bn. marched to IVERGNY at short notice. Parade 8-30 a.m. all in billets 4-0 p.m. 2nd Bn. The Worcestershire Regt. in billets near us at LE SOUICH. 2/Lt. FELLOWS A.S. joined Battalion.	
			Total Casualties to date.	
				Officers	Other Ranks
			Killed	4	96
			Wounded	12	455
			Died of Wounds	1	15
			Died of Sickness	2	6
			Missing		1

A.R. Holman

2449 Wt. W14957/M90 750,000 1/16 J.B.C. & A. Forms/C.2118/12.

Army Form C. 2118.

WAR DIARY
or
INTELLIGENCE SUMMARY
(Erase heading not required.)

1/7 Worcester Regt
Vol 2.0

Place	Date 1916 October	Hour	Summary of Events and Information	Remarks and references to Appendices
IVERGNY	1		Sudden order to move to HAILLOY received at 9·0 a.m. Parade 10·15 a.m. all in billets 1·30 p.m.	
HAILLOY	2		Companies at disposal of O.C. Coys for day training.	
	3		do.	
	4		do.	
	5		do.	
	6		Working party – 20 Officers 500 men under Major TOMKINSON to SAILLY-AU-BOIS in Motor busses to dig cable trench. Party started 12 noon and returned 8·15 p.m.	
	7		Companies at disposal of O.C. Coys. Battalion paraded 2·0 p.m. and proceeded A & C Coys to SOUASTRE B & D and Bn. H.Qrs to FONQUEVILLERS taking over at Infantry place from Major and 2 Reserve Coys of 4th Bn The Royal Warwickshire Regt. whose Companies in the Trenches were relieved by 4th Bn. The Gloucestershire Regt.	
FONQUEVILLERS	8		B & D Coys moved up from SOUASTRE and took over from 2 left Coys of 4th Bn. The Gloucestershire Regiment. "C" Coy in the line in 57D K.3.c.1. Bn. H.Q. numbered at E.29.d.4.2. "A" Coy in support in HEBUTERNE. Damage, relief complete 11·0 a.m. all Coys working very hard to get communication and parallels in good order for anticipated attack by 145th Infantry Brigade. Enemy very quiet.	WRS
	9		Quiet day in the afternoon enemy knocked in "THORPE STREET"	
	10		Early morning enemy shelled HEBUTERNE with gas shells + Heavies quiet	
	11		Quiet day. During Villa Tour goat patrol went out done by Lts. CARTER, HUMPHRIES, & LEAKE.	
	12		Bn. relieved by 6th Bn Royal Warwickshire Regt. relief complete 12 noon Battalion to billets in ST. AMAND	
	13		Battalion paraded 2·0 p.m. and marched to HUMBERCOURT where billets were taken over from 6th Glos. all in billets 5·0 p.m. Capt ADSHEAD to England.	11·20
HUMBERCOURT	14		Companies at disposal of O.C. Coys	
	15		Church parade 11·0 a.m.	
	16		Coys at disposal of O.C. Coys	
	17		do.	
	18		C.O. on leave. B & D Coys marched for CHATEAU DE LA HAIE [57] D.J.6.b] at 1·0 p.m.	

Army Form C. 2118.

WAR DIARY
or
INTELLIGENCE SUMMARY
(Erase heading not required.)

Instructions regarding War Diaries and Intelligence Summaries are contained in F. S. Regs., Part II. and the Staff Manual respectively. Title Pages will be prepared in manuscript.

Place	Date	Hour	Summary of Events and Information	Remarks and references to Appendices
	(October 1916)			
HUMEROEUIL	19 (cont'd)	2-0 p.m.	Orders received to march 2 Coys to SOUASTRE. 3-15 p.m. "A" & "C" Coys paraded ready to move but simultaneously Bn. O.O. was received which made it clear that the 2 Coys intended for SOUASTRE were those who had sent out for CHATEAU-DE-LA-HAIE and ultimately remained the night there. Remainder of the Bn. prepared to move to SAILLY-AU-BOIS on 19th inst in relief of 7th Yorkshire Regiment. "A" & "C" Coys to move at same time to HEBUTERNE in relief of same Battalion.	
			All orders cancelled by B.D Coys rejoining the Bn. about 5-0 p.m.	
	20		Battalion marched to IVERGNY. All in 11-30 a.m. Same billets as on night 30th Sept.	
IVERGNY	21		C.O's marching order inspection.	
	22		Coys at disposal of O.C. Coys.	
	23		Coys at disposal of O.C. Coys. Lt HUMPHRIES to England.	
	24		Transport & Lewis gunners moved 9-30 a.m. to TALMAS area.	
	25		Bn. paraded 9-30 a.m. and at 9-0 a.m. two lorries (French Motor Lorries) proceeded via DOULLENS - BEAUVAL - AMIENS to BRESLE. All in billets 3-0 p.m. C.O. rejoined.	
	26		Transport from leave. Transport party arrived 6-30 p.m. Bn. attached to 15th Division for work. Paraded 9-0 a.m. and marched via ALBERT and FRICOURT to a site 57 C.X.22 d. near CONTALMAISON. No tents available till 5-30 p.m. except a dozen by courtesy of O.C. 9th Bn. The Gordon Highlanders.	

Army Form C. 2118.

WAR DIARY
or
INTELLIGENCE SUMMARY
(Erase heading not required.)

Instructions regarding War Diaries and Intelligence Summaries are contained in F. S. Regs., Part II. and the Staff Manual respectively. Title Pages will be prepared in manuscript.

Place	Date	Hour	Summary of Events and Information	Remarks and references to Appendices
October 1916 27c.7.22.d.	26 (contd)		Camp ultimately pitched, ample accommodation for all – very wet night.	} files
	27		Working parties 210 men, carrying and working Tramways by night.	
	28.		Working parties 278 men.	
	29		Working parties 264 " Church parade off owing to heavy rain.	
	30		Still raining. Working Parties 300 men.	
	31		Working parties 300 men – much finer weather and a drying wind.	

Instructions sign to Lieut. to

Comdg. 1/7th Bn. Worcestershire Regt.

M.21

144/8

CONFIDENTIAL

WAR DIARY Vol 21
of
17th WORCESTER REGT

From 1st to 30th Nov. 1916

(VOL XX)

Army Form C. 2118.

WAR DIARY
or
INTELLIGENCE SUMMARY
(Erase heading not required.)

Instructions regarding War Diaries and Intelligence Summaries are contained in F. S. Regs., Part II. and the Staff Manual respectively. Title Pages will be prepared in manuscript.

Place	Date	Hour	Summary of Events and Information	Remarks and references to Appendices
November	1916			
X.22.d.	1st		Working Parties 200 men	
"	2nd		" 300 men	
"	3rd		Battalion moved to SCOTS REDOUBT 57d x 21 B at 9 a.m. Accomodation very poor, consisting of dug outs, old gun pits and some tents. Working parties 150 men	
			Cars at disposal of O. C. boys	
X.21.B.	4th		Battalion relieved 4th Bn Gloucestershire Regt.	
	5th		B.H.Q at S. E. 9. 79 (57 C) A and C Coys at STARFISH TRENCH M 33 B. B Coy at SWANSEA TRENCH S. 2. a	SW

2449 Wt. W14957/M90 750,000 1/16 J.B.C. & A. Forms/C.2118/12.

Army Form C. 2118.

WAR DIARY
or
INTELLIGENCE SUMMARY
(Erase heading not required.)

Instructions regarding War Diaries and Intelligence Summaries are contained in F. S. Regs., Part II. and the Staff Manual respectively. Title Pages will be prepared in manuscript.

Place	Date	Hour	Summary of Events and Information	Remarks and references to Appendices
	November 1916			
X 21 b	5th		D Coy at "Swansea TRENCH" S.3.c. Relief complete by 5.30 P.M. Working Party - 100 men	
S.8.a.19	6th		H.Q. shelled 12.45 - 1.30 P.M. Battalion relieved 4th Bn. The Gloucestershire Regt. B H.Q. at MARTINPUICH. A and C Coys in PRUE TRENCH 57.C. M.33.f. D in CRESCENT ALLEY M.27.d. B Coy in O.G.1 M.22.a. Relief complete 6 p.m. Working parties 500 men	SW
Martinpuich	7th 8th 9th		Battalion was relieved by 6th Bn. Royal Warwickshire Regt.	

2449 Wt. W14957/M90 750,000 1/16 J.B.C. & A. Forms/C.2118/12.

WAR DIARY
or
INTELLIGENCE SUMMARY
(Erase heading not required.)

Army Form C. 2118.

Place	Date	Hour	Summary of Events and Information	Remarks and references to Appendices
MARTINPUICH	November 1916 9th		33rd moved to PEAKE WOOD CAMP (CENTRAL) 57d × 22d. Bn reported incident 11/im	
X 22d	10th		Coys at disposal of O.C. Coys for cleaning, inspections etc	
"	11th		Coys at disposal of O.C. Coys. Working Parties 300 men	
"	12th		Church Parade (Brigade) Working Parties 200 men	
"	13th		Coys at disposal of O.C. Coys. A & C Coys practised form of attack. Working Parties 250 men	
"	14th		Coys at disposal of O.C. Coys. B & D Coys practised form of attack. Working Parties 250 men	
"	15th		Coys at disposal of O.C. Coys. Working Parties 300 men	
"	16th		Coys at disposal of O.C. Coys. Working Parties 300 men	
"	17th		Coys at disposal of O.C. Coys	
"	18th		Battalion relieved 6th Bn. Northumberland Fusiliers. B.H.Q at M2d 4.2. A Coy H.Q. M17 C 35. D Coy M17 C 35. B Coy H.Q at M22 d 9.7	

WAR DIARY
or
INTELLIGENCE SUMMARY
(Erase heading not required.)

Army Form C. 2118.

Place	Date	Hour	Summary of Events and Information	Remarks and references to Appendices
Nov 1916 X.22.d	18th		C Coy H.Q. at M.22 d 61. Line held from a line on the right drawn through M.17 Central to M 29 C.10. On left line drawn from M.16 b. 73 — M.22 c 85.00. The line held by two Coys in front position dislocated in depth one Coy in support and one in reserve. Relief completed 1.45 a.m on 19th though heavy enemy barrage during relief, no casualties. Situation reported all quiet though enemy shelled whole front.	
M.22.d.42	19th		Intermittently during the day	
M.22.d.42	20th		H.Q. Coy moved to M 22 d 61. Intermittent shelling along the front and B. H.Q shelled from 2.30 pm – 5 pm. Battalion relieved by 8th Bn Gloucestershire Regt. Relief completedly 9.45. One man killed during relief. Battalion moved to support. Bn H.Qr at "Seven Elms" M.28 d.36.	

Army Form C. 2118.

WAR DIARY
or
INTELLIGENCE SUMMARY

(Erase heading not required.)

Instructions regarding War Diaries and Intelligence Summaries are contained in F. S. Regs., Part II. and the Staff Manual respectively. Title Pages will be prepared in manuscript.

Place	Date	Hour	Summary of Events and Information	Remarks and references to Appendices
	November 1916.			
M.22.d.2	20th		A and D Coy in Pune Trench. B Coy in "STARFISH" and C Coy in RUTHERFORD ALLEY	
M.2.s.d.36	21st		Situation reported all quiet.	
"	22nd		Situation reported all quiet. Working Parties 275.	
"	23rd		Enemy shelled MARTINPUICH with Lachrymatory shells at 9 p.m. Situation all quiet. Relieved by 1/8 The Royal Warwickshire Regt. Relief completed 8.20 p.m. Battalion moved to GORDON CAMP X.16.d.90	(two)
X.16.d.90	24th		All ranks present 12.30 a.m. 24th. Coys at the disposal of C.C. Coys.	
	25th		Coys at the disposal of C.C. Coys. Working Parties 400 men	
	26th		Working Parties 220 men	
	27th		Working Parties 220 men	

Army Form C. 2118.

WAR DIARY
or
INTELLIGENCE SUMMARY
(Erase heading not required.)

Instructions regarding War Diaries and Intelligence Summaries are contained in F.S. Regs., Part II. and the Staff Manual respectively. Title Pages will be prepared in manuscript.

Place	Date	Hour	Summary of Events and Information	Remarks and references to Appendices
Thorneby	November 1916			
X16 d90	28th		Battalion moved to "SHELTERWOOD CAMP SOUTH" X 21 d. Camp unfinished but all men under cover by dark. Working parties 220 men Boys at disposal of C.C. Boys for improvement of Huteuets 230 men.	
X 21 d	29th		Working Parties. Boys at disposal of C.C. Boys. Working parties 270 men	
"	30th			

Total Casualties for month.

	Officers	Other Ranks
Killed	—	7
Wounded	—	13
Died of Wounds	—	1

M.A. Mackenzie Lieut. Col.
Comdg. 1/7th Bn. Worcestershire Regt.

Vol 22

11/22

Confidential

War Diary
of
1/4th Worcestershire Regiment

from 1st December 1916 to 31st December 1916.

Volume 21

WAR DIARY or INTELLIGENCE SUMMARY

Army Form C. 2118.

Place	Date	Hour	Summary of Events and Information	Remarks and references to Appendices
Trenches (N.A.6) Sq. 22.d.6.1.	1/9/16		Battalion relieved the 1/4th Bn. The Royal Warwickshire Regt. Bn. H.Q. at M.22.d.6.1. A Coy H.Q. at M.22.c.35. C.Coy H.Q. M.22.a.97. B Coy H.Q. N.22.d.61. Relief complete 7.40pm. Situation normal but our guns fired short at 3.25am. One of our own shells fell in a set of M.P.C.79. Killed 1 man and wounded two others. Situation reported normal. Good band work being done by Lt. PARKE & 2/Lt ALLEN also by 2/Lt WALLACE. Our artillery fire slit during day.	ALR
	3rd		At 4.0 am a fighting patrol 'A' Co. 2/Lt WALLACE raided a German post at M.P.c.65. Party was divided in fire. 2/Lt WALLACE with 5 other ranks reached the post and inflicted several casualties but owing to the heavy going the night being arrived late. Having all raids 2/Lt WALLACE 2529 Sergt, 3mo. A.H. 3169 Corpl. Cpl. H. Thomas & Pte. J. Wilks behaved very gallantly.	
	4th		Enemy retired to good cover but inflicted some casualties during relocating 2/Lt Timbrell was in charge of the covering party which did good work in evacuating the casualties. L.Coy. relieved A.Coy. and then relieved A.Coy. Relief complete 8.40.am. 10.30. The 10/Chesh & 1/5 S.W.B. Regiment awarded by Corps Commander for diversion to July on 19th Nov 16. Situation reported normal. Our artillery again firing short killing one man in MAXWELL TRENCH.	
	5th		Bn. relieved by 1/4th Bn. The Royal Warwickshire Regt. Relief complete by 10.3pm. Bn. moved to VILLA CAMP north of Bn. camps Sq. D.A.11.6.	
Sq. D.A.11.6	6th		Remained at disposal of Corps.	

WAR DIARY or INTELLIGENCE SUMMARY

Army Form C. 2118.

Place	Date	Hour	Summary of Events and Information	Remarks and references to Appendices
Sq.P.x.11.c.	1916 6th		Companies at disposal of O.C.s in camp for movement. Permanent working Coy. 80 men formed.	
	7th		Companies at disposal of O.C.s in camp for movement.	
	9th		Bn. relieved 1st K.R.R. Royal Warwickshire Regt. in support trenches. B.H.Q. at Devon Ave. N: 29 d. 36. Coys in same disposition as K.R.R. A & D. in PRUE TRENCH. B in STARFISH. & C. in RUTHERFORD ALLEY.	
N: 26.a.36	10th		Working party 90 men.	B.H.Q. comp. coy. 9.30 a.m. and relieved BUTTE ALLEY
	11th		Working party 200 men 2/Lt. Campbell & 20 O.R. to holding BUTTE TRENCH BUTTE ALLEY & be wired and strongly held.	
	12th		Relieved by 1st Bn. Gloucestershire Regt. in front line. B.H.Q. at M.r. c. 3.3. D.Coy. H.Q. m. 22. d. 91. A.Coy. H.Q. to 22 d 81. Bn. H.Q. at m. 22. d. 81. Relief complete 9 p.m.	
Bn. 22.d.81.	13th		Everything normal. nothing to report.	
	14th		Relieved by 7.6 K.O.S.B. Relief complete by 9. a.s.m. Bn. moved to MIDDLE WOOD camp. K. 12. c. 31.	
N. 12. c.21.	15th		Coys at disposal of O.C. Coys.	
	16th		Bn. moved to ALBERT. Billets Accommodation good.	
ALBERT	17th		Coys at disposal of O.C. Coys.	
	18th		Coys at disposal of O.C. Coys.	
	19th		Coys at disposal of O.C. Coys. in Rugger, Drill, musketry, Route March, Lecturing var. 6.30 min	
	20th		Coys at disposal of O.C. Coys in P.T. Musketry, & Route March. combine bath. 150 men	
	21st		Coy at disposal of O.C. Coys to O.C. Bayont lighting. & Route March. working party 90 m.m.	
	22nd		Coy at disposal of	
	23rd		Corporals at disposal of O.C. Coys. P.T. & Bayonet lighting route march.	

Army Form C. 2118.

WAR DIARY
or
INTELLIGENCE SUMMARY

(Erase heading not required.)

Instructions regarding War Diaries and Intelligence Summaries are contained in F. S. Regs., Part II. and the Staff Manual respectively. Title Pages will be prepared in manuscript.

Place	Date	Hour	Summary of Events and Information	Remarks and references to Appendices
ALBERT.	24.7.		Divine service. Church parade.	
	25.7.		Holiday. 1st Platoon of Co. in Squad drill. Bayonet fighting & route march.	
	26.7.		Coys. at disposal of OC Coys. in extended order drill. Bayonet fighting & route march.	Letter
	27.7.		Bn. moved to MILLENCOURT. Brady for 1.50.p. under canvas.	
	28.7.		Coys. at disposal of O.C. Coys in P.T. Squad drills. Bayonet fighting & Musketry.	
MILLENCOURT.	29.7.		Bn. moved from MILLENCOURT to BAIZIEUX. Billetted in huts accommodation good.	
	30.7.		Church parade under Coy. arrangements. Lt. Col. TOMKINSON rejoined from leave.	
BAIZIEUX.	31.7.		Total casualties to date.	
				Officers. Other Ranks.
			Killed.	1. 6.
			Died of wounds.	1. 16.
			Died of sickness.	2. 2.
			Wounded.	12. 491.
			Missing.	1. 2.
			Prisoners of war.	1. 2.

J.H. Tomkinson Lieut. Col.
Comdg. 1/7th Bn. Worcestershire Regt.

M 23

Confidential

1/4 or 1st installment 10/-
to be due January 1911
(Return XXII)

Army Form C. 2118.

WAR DIARY
or
INTELLIGENCE SUMMARY
(Erase heading not required.)

Instructions regarding War Diaries and Intelligence Summaries are contained in F. S. Regs., Part II. and the Staff Manual respectively. Title Pages will be prepared in manuscript.

Place	Date	Hour	Summary of Events and Information	Remarks and references to Appendices
BAIZIEUX	January 1		Coys at dispost 2.0 Coys for P.E Bayonet training Extended order and march	
			one at dispost & C.6 Coys for R.E. Bayonet fighting & Lewis	
	2		Presented the M.B.M. to one Jones a.r. L.E. Coy in the afternoon the Brigade Commander	
			Coys training in R.E. Bayonet fighting, Lewis Guns, firing on the range.	
	3		The following rewards were announced in Brigade Orders Extracted from London Gazette £.1.12.00	
			Jan 1. M. Col. J.H. Tomkinson - - - D.S.O.	
			Lt. P. Barber - - - M.C.	
			Lt. G.L. Dixon - - - M.E	
			Lt. Richfield to be Hony Captain.	
	4		Owing to the rain the route march was cancelled & troops were given serious & indoor instruction.	
	5		Coys at the disposal of Coys for Musket training, Bayonet fighting and drill.	
	6		The Battalion was inspected in the afternoon by the Corps Commander Lt Gen Pulteney.	
			Owing to the mud they Coys were their Great coats. The 8 Worcesters were inspected at the	
			same time. Inspection ground - BAIZIEUX.	
	7		The Battalion paraded for Divine Service in the morning. In the Afternoon orders received	
			about 11. A.M. that at 3 o'clock next morning the Bn. to proceed to HUPPY	
			by route march and train.	
	8		The Battalion left BAIZIEUX at 3. o'clock in the morning & marched to HEILLY station where	
			it entrained. At 7. am the train moved off & arrived at PONT REMY at 10.30 a.m.	
			The troops were served out with Coffee & the Bn. marched to HUPPY 5 miles & arrived in the	

2449 Wt. W14957/M99 750,000 1/16 J.B.C. & A. Forms/C.2118/12.

Army Form C. 2118.

WAR DIARY
or
INTELLIGENCE SUMMARY

(Erase heading not required.)

Instructions regarding War Diaries and Intelligence Summaries are contained in F. S. Regs., Part II. and the Staff Manual respectively. Title Pages will be prepared in manuscript.

Place	Date	Hour	Summary of Events and Information	Remarks and references to Appendices
HOPPE	January 28th		Bn. paraded 11 am marched to PONT REMY, entrained at 1.0 pm arrived CERISY 12 midnight. Bn. billetted in village all in by 2.30 a.m. Transport arrived CERISY at 7 am and marched onwards.	
CERISY	29		Billets for all disposed of & large	
	30		accn. at disposal of A Coy.	
	31		Coys on short route march & arms billet drill.	

[signature] Lieut. Col.
Comdg. 1/7th Bn. Worcestershire Regt.

Mrs Thomas

M.24

Vol 24

Experimental

War Diary

of

1/4th Bn Worcestershire Regt.

July 1st to Feby 26th 1917.

(VOL XXIII)

Army Form C. 2118.

WAR DIARY
or
INTELLIGENCE SUMMARY
(Erase heading not required.)

Instructions regarding War Diaries and Intelligence Summaries are contained in F. S. Regs., Part II. and the Staff Manual respectively. Title Pages will be prepared in manuscript.

Place	Date	Hour	Summary of Events and Information	Remarks and references to Appendices
CAPPY	1917 Feb. 1.		The Batt.n marched from CERISY to CAPPY, a distance of about 9 miles	
TRENCHES	2.		The Batt.n proceeded to take up a position in SUPPORT TRENCHES at H 35 d. The trenches were taken over from the FRENCH, the 135 Reg.t Infanterie.	
	3.		The Batt.n remained in SUPPORT	
	4.		In SUPPORT 2nd Lt C.C Underwood, attached to 8th Batt.n R Worcestershire Reg.t Killed in action	
	5.	do	During the night the enemy made a determined raid on the 1/6 Gloucester Reg.t & the FRENCH on their RIGHT. Our Batt.n was not touched. The raid was unsuccessful, but the trenches were much damaged by the barrage	4. O.R. wounded.
	6.	do	Working Parties sent to help to repair trenches damaged by the raid.	
	7.		The Batt.n took over the front system of Trenches from the 1/6 Gloucester Reg.t	2/Lieut. A.J. DAVIES wounded.
	8.		In Trenches. A fairly quiet day.	
	9.		Batt.n relieved by the 1/5 Gloucester Reg.t & march to CAPPY	1. O.R. wounded
CAPPY	10		In billets Companies placed at the disposal of O.C Coys.	
	11		Divine Service in morning. In the evening during Roll Call a fire suddenly broke out in the Billet occupied by C & D Coys. So rapidly did it spread that nothing could be done to save the building & much equipment was destroyed	

2449 Wt. W14957/M90 750,000 1/16 J.B.C. & A. Forms/C.2118/12.

Army Form C. 2118.

WAR DIARY
or
INTELLIGENCE SUMMARY
(Erase heading not required.)

Instructions regarding War Diaries and Intelligence Summaries are contained in F.S. Regs., Part II. and the Staff Manual respectively. Title Pages will be prepared in manuscript.

Place	Date	Hour	Summary of Events and Information	Remarks and references to Appendices
CAPPY	1917 Feb. 12		Companies were placed at the disposal of O.C. Companies for platoon training. A bombing class was also commenced. Billets were inspected by the Commanding Officer.	
	13		Companies placed at the disposal of O.C. Companies for platoon training & bombing.	
	14		Platoon training continued. Inspection of Officers reserves. Classes for Officers by the Medical Officer for instruction in the use of the Box Respirator.	
	15		Coys placed at the disposal of O.C. Coys for instruction in the use of the Box Respirator, & for Route March by platoons.	
	16		Coys. placed at the disposal of O.C. Coys for further instruction in the Box Respirator, & for intensive economy. All men paraded for the new Trench Foot Treatment.	
	17		The Batt. relieved the 1/4 Batt. Oxford & Bucks Regt. on as Support Battn. to the Right Brigade, occupy taking over the trenches in H 35 a	
TRENCHES	18		In SUPPORT. Working parties busy improving & strengthening dugouts & making footboards	
	19		In support. Work on dugouts continued	

WAR DIARY
or
INTELLIGENCE SUMMARY
(Erase heading not required.)

Army Form C. 2118.

Instructions regarding War Diaries and Intelligence Summaries are contained in F.S. Regs., Part II. and the Staff Manual respectively. Title Pages will be prepared in manuscript.

Place	Date	Hour	Summary of Events and Information	Remarks and references to Appendices
TRENCHES	1917 Feb. 20		In SUPPORT. Work on dug-outs continued. The thaw & rain gradually converting the Trenches into a state of collapse.	
	21		The Batt. at dusk relieved the 16th Gloucestershire Regt in the front line. Three Coys holding the front line :- B on Left, A in Centre, & C on Right. The night was extremely dark & much of the relief was done on the lid owing to the terrible state of the Trenches. The relief by A Coy was done splendidly. B & C were not so fortunate & many men were stuck in the mud & had to be helped out. The relief was not completed until after midnight. A patrol was sent out by D Coy, but the intense darkness stopped much success. The functioning was not easy. Our front showed by Trench Mortars. Ration Parties had great difficulty in moving. 3 O.R. killed. 1 O.R. wounded.	
	22			
	23		During the day our Right Coy was troubled a good deal by minenwerfers & aerial darts. The artillery was fairly quiet during the day. About 7.45 p.m. heavy bombardment was heard far away to our RIGHT, this gradually worked away towards us & at last reached our RIGHT Coy. Our front & support lines were shelled severely for some time but there was no Infantry action. After lasting half an hour the shelling gradually ceased & the night was quiet. 1 O.R. killed. 1 O.R. D.f.W. 9 O.R. wounded.	
	24	a.m. 5.50	At 5.50 a.m. an intense bombardment of our front & support lines began. Our Posts 10, 11 (a Lewis Gun Post), 9/12 on the LEFT of our RIGHT Coy saw about 10 men leave the German Sap at N12 & 4, 3 & approach our lines under the barrage. Fire was opened up & a Bangalore M.G. between posts 11 & 12 also started. Our Post No. 11 was wrecked by a great explosion. 1 O.R. missing. 5 O.R. wounded.	

Army Form C. 2118.

WAR DIARY
or
INTELLIGENCE SUMMARY

(Erase heading not required.)

Instructions regarding War Diaries and Intelligence Summaries are contained in F. S. Regs., Part II. and the Staff Manual respectively. Title Pages will be prepared in manuscript.

Place	Date	Hour	Summary of Events and Information	Remarks and references to Appendices
TRENCHES	1917 February 24	5.50 a.m	1 of our sentry was killed whilst the other was wounded. The Lewis Gun was blown up.	
		6.30	The guns became quiet & the bombardment, which had worked to our LEFT, ceased. During the day it was observed that two new German dead lay in front of the point of trench which had been raided. A patrol was therefore sent out at night to secure identification. It was successful & brought back the discs of one of the men, which was at once sent to BRIGADE. Our casualties very small considering the violence of the barrage, & not much damage was done to the Trenches. Owing to roads being jammed on the act. & the wide trenches being bridged in many cases the carrying parties had much easier taats this night.	
	25		The mist at last cleared today, & towards midday the sun came out & the first enemy planes for a week came over our lines flying low. In the evening the Battn was relieved by the 1/5 Gloucestershire Regt & went back to the dugouts in the SUPPORT LINE. It was a very good relief & was completed by 9.5 p.m, our guides working well. 3 O.R. wounded. 1 O.R. missing. 3 O.R. wounded.	

2449 Wt. W14957/M90 750,000 1/16 J.B.C. & A. Forms/C.2118/12.

Army Form C. 2118.

WAR DIARY
or
INTELLIGENCE SUMMARY
(Erase heading not required.)

Instructions regarding War Diaries and Intelligence Summaries are contained in F.S. Regs., Part II. and the Staff Manual respectively. Title Pages will be prepared in manuscript.

Place	Date	Hour	Summary of Events and Information	Remarks and references to Appendices
TRENCHES	1917 Feb 26		The men were rested today in the SUPPORT LINE, only small working parties being found. At 6 p.m. the Battn was relieved by the 1/1 Bucks. Regt. & marched back to the old billets at CAPPY. The men marched splendidly.	
CAPPY	27		The day was spent in cleaning & tending to feet, the men parading for TRENCH FOOT Treatment. A Board of Enquiry was held today at Battn. H.Q. to enquire into the circumstances of the fire at the Pilots of C & D Coys which happened on the night of the 11th inst.	
	28		A working party from D Coy of 100 men was found in the morning to go to the BOIS de MEREAUCOURT (east of FRISE) & another of 400 set out in the afternoon to go to ACHILLE RAVINE to work on trench-cleaning. Casualties for the month. 5. O.R. Killed. 1. Officer Killed. 3. O.R. D. of Wounds. 1 " wounded 20. O.R. wounded. 2. O.R. missing.	

J.H.Wilkinson Lieut. Col.
Comdg. 1/7th Bn. Worcestershire Regt.

Confidential   Vol 25

1/7th Bn. Worcestershire Regiment

Mrs Brown Ⓢ   U.25

WAR DIARY FOR MARCH 1917

VOLUME 24.

Army Form C. 2118.

WAR DIARY
or
INTELLIGENCE SUMMARY.
(Erase heading not required.)

Instructions regarding War Diaries and Intelligence Summaries are contained in F. S. Regs. Part II. and the Staff Manual respectively. Title pages will be prepared in manuscript.

Place	Date	Hour	Summary of Events and Information	Remarks and references to Appendices
CAPPY	1917 March 1		Working parties were found by the Battⁿ as follows:— 1 Capt + 100 O.R. on clearing O.Ts at H 20 6 22. 1 Capt + 250 O.R. on track laying at H 36 c 33	
"	2		One working party of 1 Off + 50 O.R. found to work in forward area. The remainder of the men was sent to the baths	
"	3		The Battⁿ relieved the 1/5 Gloucestershire Reg⁺ + 1 Coy 4th R Berkshire Reg⁺ at dusk. Dispositions — B + C in front line, D on left + C on Right, with A + D in support in ACHILL'S RAVINE 2 n/c.o/⁺ NESS + 11 O.R. of B Coy were wounded by shrapnel during the relief, on the FLAUCOURT - BIACHES R⁴. One man of A Coy was wounded on carrying party	
In Trenches	4		Enemy Artillery + Aeroplane active. No casualties	
"	5		A fairly quiet day. 1 OR B Coy wounded. In evening A relieved B + D relieved C in front line	
"	6		Nothing of interest to report. No casualties	
"	7		Relieved in evening by 1/5 Gloucestershire Reg⁺ + 1/1 Bucks Battⁿ. A good relief was made + the Battⁿ arrived in billets at 12.45 AM. Casualties — 2 OR killed + 1 OR wounded	
CAPPY	8		Coys. finished off Anti-Trench Foot Baths. B + C sent to baths at FROISSY	

Army Form C. 2118.

WAR DIARY
of
INTELLIGENCE SUMMARY.
(Erase heading not required.)

Instructions regarding War Diaries and Intelligence Summaries are contained in F. S. Regs., Part II. and the Staff Manual respectively. Title pages will be prepared in manuscript.

Place	Date	Hour	Summary of Events and Information	Remarks and references to Appendices
SUPPORT TRENCHES	1917 March 17	2.30am	The 14th Bde. attack LA MAISONETTE & found Bde. opposition. All opposition taken. Two passages from our Bat?? assist by enemy laying traps & cutting wires, & also by taking up & laying scaling ladders. A & B stand to all night ready to carry forward bombs & rations, but do not get orders until 6 am when a party of B Coy is found to carry forward finding that the Germans are evacuating their trench system WEST of the River the 6th Gloster & 8th Worcester push forward platoons to occupy the German front line. No opposition. At dusk the Bat?? took over the new positions taken up by the 6th Gloucesters, the dispositions were :— C on right, A on left with B in support & D in reserve. Front held from N.12.c.4.1. to O.2.c.05.70. Before this, light pulled an Officers patrol under 2 2/Lt Clark detailed to canal bank & from LA CHAPELETTE to ETERPIGNY without finding any Germans. At 6 pm two standing patrols are sent out to guard the river crossings at O.3.d.3.2 & LAMIRE FARM.	
TRENCHES & OUTPOSTS	18		D Coy push forward when light fails & take up an outpost line on the western bank of the river SOMME. The front being from O.3.G.5.O. to the outskirts of ETERPIGNY. Sentry groups were placed along the canal bank & the picquet line along FOURCH – APOLLO – PAQUE 70. Coy HQ at GARDEN FARM. Other dispositions :— A Coy on O.G.1.9.2., B Coy in CENTRE – PIGAL – MAUFOIL & POMMIERS, & C Coy in CHEMINADE. Bat?? HQ in Front Bat?? HQ. The day was absolutely quiet & reports showed that the enemy was EAST of the River only.	

(A3092.) W. W.12859/M.1293. 75,0.0. 1/17. D. D. & L., Ltd. Forms/C.2118/14.

Army Form C. 2118.

WAR DIARY
or
INTELLIGENCE SUMMARY.
(Erase heading not required.)

Instructions regarding War Diaries and Intelligence Summaries are contained in F. S. Regs., Part II. and the Staff Manual respectively. Title pages will be prepared in manuscript.

Place	Date	Hour	Summary of Events and Information	Remarks and references to Appendices
OUTPOST POSITION	1917 March 19	5 am	Lt PEARE & 30 men of D Coy with great difficulty crossed the broken bridge at LANIRE FARM & take up a position in the vicinity of O 11 Central, with scouty groups at EASTERN entrance to LE MESNIL. Similar action taken by the 1st Division on our Right & the 4th Division on our Left. These operations quite successfully carried out & no enemy encountered.	
		6 pm	B Coy take over D Coy's positions.	
	20	5.30 am	B Coy move forward across the river to LE MESNIL	
		8.45 am	B Coy report that Coy HQ have been established in LE MESNIL & that piquets are being placed in position. Also that CARTIGNY has been patrolled & found free of the enemy.	
		9.15 am	B Coy report that piquets are established at :— P/13 a 2, & P 7 a 2 7.	
		10 am	Orders received that the remainder of the Battn is to move to LE MESNIL	
		afternoon	Battn HQ takes up its position in LE MESNIL & A & D in good billets in the village (in dug outs & cellars) C Coy goes forward & takes over the piquet line from B Coy who return to billets in the village. All night position found to mend the ruined cross-roads.	

Army Form C. 2118.

WAR DIARY
or
INTELLIGENCE SUMMARY.
(Erase heading not required.)

Instructions regarding War Diaries and Intelligence Summaries are contained in F. S. Regs., Part II. and the Staff Manual respectively. Title pages will be prepared in manuscript.

Place	Date	Hour	Summary of Events and Information	Remarks and references to Appendices
PERONNE	1917 March 26		Day spent in cleaning billets.	
	27		Working parties were found as follows :—	
			2 Offrs & 80 OR to report at 12 & 61 for road mending	
			2 Offrs & 80 OR " X Roads J19a do	
			2 OR " 130 co1 for filling in mine craters in road.	
			2 Offrs & 80 OR " X Roads J21a for road making & crater filling	
			2 Offrs & 120 OR " J 33 a 20 for damming river	
			20 OR " BUIRE Church for filling carts	
	28		Working parties as yesterday.	
	29		The usual working parties are found, but have to be recalled at midday owing to orders being received for a sudden move to TINCOURT. The Battn moves away at 3 p.m. & arrives at 5 p.m. to the village finding fairly good billets there. The march was done in very heavy rain.	
TINCOURT	30		Small parties on cleaning roads & billets in morning. At 6 p.m. the Battn is ordered to move at once to SAULCOURT WOOD & starts away at 10 p.m. arriving in the WOOD after midnight. No tents or friends & men have to make room for the night as best they could.	

WAR DIARY
or
INTELLIGENCE SUMMARY.
(Erase heading not required.)

Army Form C. 2118.

Place	Date	Hour	Summary of Events and Information	Remarks and references to Appendices
SAULCOURT WOOD	1917 March 31.		At 3 p.m. two platoons of C. Coy. advanced towards EPEHY with the object of feeling the strength of its garrison. As soon as they came into observation over the ridge by CAPRON COPSE they were heavily shelled & lose 4 killed & 7 wounded. They take cover in a sunken road until darkness comes on & then push on to the Elm trees on the sunken road from VILLERS FAUCON — EPEHY, there they dig in for the night & encounter no further signs of the enemy. Casualties for the month. 1 Officer & 2 N.C.O.s & 3 wounded. Killed in action. 5. Wnd & wounds. 1. Wounded in action. 28.	

J Townsend ?
Lieut. Col.
Commdg. 1/7th Bn. Worcestershire Regt.

M.26

144/48 Vol 26

Confidential

War Diary
of
H.Q. the Worcestershire Bde.

From 1/4/17 to 30/4/17

(vol XXIV)

Army Form C. 2118.

WAR DIARY
or
INTELLIGENCE SUMMARY.
(Erase heading not required.)

Instructions regarding War Diaries and Intelligence Summaries are contained in F.S. Regs., Part II. and the Staff Manual respectively. Title pages will be prepared in manuscript.

Place	Date	Hour	Summary of Events and Information	Remarks and references to Appendices
EPEHY	1917 April 1		Operations against EPEHY	
		2 a.m	Batt. moved off from SAULCOURT WOOD to form up for the attack	
		5 a.m	Advance on the village commenced.	
		5.45 a.m	The leading Platoons enter the village. The enemy was completely surprised & did not realise anything wrong until we were about 50 yds from the village. At then opened up rifle & machine gun fire & a weak barrage. The latter fell well behind the advancing troops.	
		6 a.m	The South end of the village reached. Well formed trench assaulted by MALASSISE FARM. The guns were turned on this FARM & opposition ceased.	
			The barrage moved to the S.W. end of the village & shelled heavily. The S. end of the village & F7a was shelled most severely.	
		6.45 a.m	The dispositions at this time were — B. Coy finally at Railway in F1b; A Coy. partly in F1b & partly in F1d, D Coy on a trench in F1c 7.F1d	
		7.15 a.m	Batt. H Q formed on trench in F1c 3d. The village was now completely cleared & thereafter avoided as much as possible.	
		8.00 a.m	Dispositions at this time were — Observation post at MALASSISE FARM, one platoon at F1d.31, at 4/d.9.0 a post; two platoons at F.1a 7.6, one platoon on railway in F1b. Two platoons in trench in F1c.3.2, two platoons in trench F12 U & one Coy on sunken road running SW to NE in E 12	

Army Form C. 2118.

WAR DIARY
or
INTELLIGENCE SUMMARY.
(Erase heading not required.)

Instructions regarding War Diaries and Intelligence Summaries are contained in F. S. Regs., Part II. and the Staff Manual respectively. Title pages will be prepared in manuscript.

Place	Date	Hour	Summary of Events and Information	Remarks and references to Appendices
EPEHY	April 1917 1 (cont'd)		During day the shelling of EPEHY was intermittent. D Coy were gradually withdrawn to support, took on E.12.b. In the evening B'n H.Q. was moved to F.7.a.a & C Coy took over the line held by the 8th Gloucesters. During the operations 1 Machine gun & 2 Lewis guns were captured by A Coy & 17 dead Germans were counted in our area together with much equipment. At night One Platoon of D Coy was sent out to consolidate MALASSISE FARM & patrols were pushed out to keep in touch with the enemy. Casualties during the day :— 1 Officer (2/Lt Felton) & 9 OR killed & 40 OR wounded.	
	2		The day was somewhat quieter. Towards dusk the Front Line & MALASSISE FARM were heavily shelled. At dusk the two front Coys were relieved by the two remaining Coys without incident.	
	3		The shelling was much less violent during this day. The Bat'n was relieved at night by 1/5 Gloucesters. The Coys on final relief marched back via SAILLCOURT WOOD to billets in HAMEL.	
HAMEL	4		The day was spent on resting & cleaning up.	

WAR DIARY
or
INTELLIGENCE SUMMARY.

(Erase heading not required.)

Army Form C. 2118.

Place	Date	Hour	Summary of Events and Information	Remarks and references to Appendices
Outpost Line	1917 April 12	(contd)	All night a very heavy musketeen made preparations for the attack very difficult	
	13		Operations against the ridge	
		3.30 a.m	The troops in position for the advance. A Coy on Right, B on Left, C & D in reserve. The attacking Coys were from our firm X roads F.29 central to GUEUDECOURT WOOD. The ground had new crater, leaving a whole ground & made movement without being seen extremely difficult	
		4.39 a.m	Forwd Enemy observed something & many lights sent up	
		3.40 a.m	Red lights sent up	
		3.45 a.m	Rifle & M.G. fire opened up by the enemy	
		3.50 a.m	The enemy put down a faint heavy barrage on the line of our forward posts. All the same time the region of the RAPARIS in F.27.a was shelled with 4.2 hour	
		4.15 a.m	The barrage quietened down a little	
		4 till 11.00	Here both Coys reached their objective. Most of the opposition was located on the right. The enemy was in considerable numbers but they did not resist much. On our troops advanced 40-50 enemy was seen retreating on the Right, priority sending up to support. A Lewis gun dispersed them & killed several	
			All 11.20 down the attacking Coys were not in touch	
		7 a.m	The enemy worked the Left flank of the Right Coy (A) & attempted to surround them. The enemy was kept by by our Lewis guns	

Army Form C. 2118.

WAR DIARY
or
INTELLIGENCE SUMMARY.
(Erase heading not required.)

Instructions regarding War Diaries and Intelligence Summaries are contained in F. S. Regs., Part II. and the Staff Manual respectively. Title pages will be prepared in manuscript.

Place	Date	Hour	Summary of Events and Information	Remarks and references to Appendices
Support Line	1917 April 13 (Good Fri)	9 a.m	Our dispositions were now — On the line F.27 d.10 — X roads F.29 a.6 central — X roads F.29 c.9.5 at a salient of the operations. 5 Prisoners & 2 M.G.s were captured by us. Estimate of Germans killed result from 12 to 50. Our casualties estimated at 6 killed & 30 wounded.	
			The afternoon passed without incident except that the neighbourhood of the RAPARIES was heavily shelled by 4.2 howr.	
		5 pm	The Left Coy reported that our Field Guns were shelling his front line.	
		6 pm	The enemy suddenly expecting a continuation of our attack, especially on our Right, put up a heavy barrage on the line roughly from F.28 c NE to F.28 b SW, it is a little in front of TOMS WOOD. He did no damage.	
		8.25 pm	The 4th Ox & Bucks began to relieve our Battn. The night was very dark, but a good way was made. Our guides working very well.	
			The relief was complete at 12.30 a.m. & the Coys as filed marched to a Camp on the Railway at M.5.b.	
In Camp	14		In Camp	
			The day was spent on rest & cleaning up.	
			ed working party of 2 Coys on the Corps line & Roads	
	15		The remainder of 4th Battn attended Church Parade at noon in the Railway Cutting near the Camp	

A3534 Wt.W4973/M687 750,000 8/16 D. D. & L. Ltd. Forms/C.2118/13.

Army Form C. 2118.

WAR DIARY
or
INTELLIGENCE SUMMARY.
(Erase heading not required.)

Instructions regarding War Diaries and Intelligence Summaries are contained in F. S. Regs., Part II. and the Staff Manual respectively. Title pages will be prepared in manuscript.

Place	Date	Hour	Summary of Events and Information	Remarks and references to Appendices
In Camp	1917 April 16.		Working parties of 3 Coys found. At 6 p.m. the Battn moved to HAMEL to take over the billets of the 1/E Yorks.	
HAMEL	17		Owing to operations by the 143 & 145 Bdes against TOMBOIS FARM & GILLEMONT FARM the Battn stood to from 4.30 a.m. to 9.30 a.m. Baths allotted to the Battn at TINCOURT In the afternoon a mine exploded in the 13" Transport Lines. Lt PEAKE & the Transport Officer 2"Lt WRIGHT were wounded & also 2 O.R. Six heavy draft, two light draft, & two mules were killed.	
	18		At 10 a.m. an order was received that B.H.Q. & all Coy H.Q. were to move into the open at once. The rest of the day was spent in constructing H.Q. huts. Two Coys were on working parties on the HAMEL - MARQUAIX Road. Baths at TINCOURT allotted to the Battn	
	19		The Battn moved to Camp near Pleasant House at E.29.c, taking over from the 1 Bucks Battn Baths at TINCOURT allotted to the Battn Two Companies at work on the TINCOURT - ROISEL Road.	

Army Form C. 2118.

WAR DIARY
or
INTELLIGENCE SUMMARY.
(Erase heading not required.)

Place	Date	Hour	Summary of Events and Information	Remarks and references to Appendices
	1917 April 20		Working parties found for road making & repairing	
	21		Parties found to collect material in ST EMILIE for making huts in the Camp.	
			Batt: moved forward at dusk to take over the front line from the 1/5 The Worcestershire Regt.	
			B Coy & A Coy taking over the Left & Right Front resp.t , D Coy in Support & C Coy in Reserve.	
			The relief was good & the night passed quietly	
	22		C Coy relieves B Coy, & D Coy relieves A Coy.	
			Careful watch was kept on GILLEMONT FARM during the day & patrolling carried out at night to gain information for the 8 Worcs, who are to attack the Farm on the morning of the 24th	
	23		The 8th Worcs. take over our positions, in order to support them our A & B Coys are left in the line, disposed as follows :—	
			A Coy – Coy H.Q. + 2 Platoons in Sunken Road at F.23.c.4.4.	
			1 Platoon in QUEUCHETTES WOOD.	
			1 Platoon in TOINE WOOD.	
			B Coy. at F.21.c.3.4.	
			C & D were withdrawn to a camp at F.25.a.8.6. & also Bn H.Q.	

WAR DIARY or INTELLIGENCE SUMMARY.

Army Form C. 2118.

(Erase heading not required.)

Instructions regarding War Diaries and Intelligence Summaries are contained in F.S. Regs., Part II. and the Staff Manual respectively. Title pages will be prepared in manuscript.

Place	Date	Hour	Summary of Events and Information	Remarks and references to Appendices
	1917 April 24		At 3.45 a.m. 4th & 9th Coys attacked GILLEMONT FARM & the high ground on A.19.a. They were driven out of their objectives by a Counter attack & Gun B&B was ordered to continue the operation the same night in conjunction with the 4 Div on the left & the 4 R. W. Regt on the right. Arrangements had to be made very hurriedly owing to the short time allowed & the Batt'n being re-assembled. Operation Orders were issued at 7 p.m. C Coy was ordered to be the Right Coy, D the Left, with B Coy in Support & A Coy in Reserve. Zero hour was to be at 11.15 p.m. B Coy, at 11.15 p.m. Zero hour, & D & B Coys reached their objectives successfully. C Coy came suffered casualties from own own barrage & then attack disorganised	
	25	6 a.m.	A heavy counter attack brought the remnants of 2 Coys. inward against our front line. Our men fell back on their second line & held it. The enemy suffered heavily, our Lewis gun & rifle fire, whilst the barrage caused great losses.	
		1.30 a.m.	A fresh counter attack on our position failed leaving the enemy things near our own line front line had	
		5.45 p.m.	The enemy put up a heavy barrage & appeared to be about to attack. Our artillery barrage fell strongly & stopped things the enemy. All night the Batt'n was relieved by the 1 Royal Irish. Casualties during the attack — Officers — 2 killed & 4 wounded O.R. — 72 killed, 90 men wounded, & 24 missing A great proportion of the wounded were probably killed in answer to gas	

Army Form C. 2118.

WAR DIARY
or
INTELLIGENCE SUMMARY.
(Erase heading not required.)

Instructions regarding War Diaries and Intelligence Summaries are contained in F. S. Regs., Part II. and the Staff Manual respectively. Title pages will be prepared in manuscript.

Place	Date	Hour	Summary of Events and Information	Remarks and references to Appendices
HAMEL	1917 April 5		Working parties found to work on CORPS LINE on K.9.6 & K.9.a.	
	6		Working parties continued.	
	7		At 6.45 p.m. the Battn moved away to take over the Outpost positions of the Left Battn of the Brigade from the 1 Bucks Battn. The route taken was through MILLERS FARCON & S2 EMILIE. Dispositions taken over:—	
			B⁺ H Q on Railway Cutting, in Tents, at F.8.C.25	
			D Coy Front over the Left Front	
			B Coy " " Right Front	
			C Coy in Support at BASSE BOULOGNE	
			A Coy in Entrenchment at F.8.c.39	
			During the night the neighbourhood of the cutting in F.8.C. was heavily shelled, 7 shells were freely sprinkled over the low ground in this district.	
	8		EASTER SUNDAY. A quiet day.	
			At night C Coy took over the Left Coy front of the 4th Gloucesters, & A relieved D.	
			Battn H Q moved to a dugout in F.13.6.79	

A 5834 Wt. W4973/M687 750,000 8/16 D. D. & L. Ltd. Forms/C2118/13.

Army Form C. 2118.

WAR DIARY
or
INTELLIGENCE SUMMARY.
(Erase heading not required.)

Instructions regarding War Diaries and Intelligence Summaries are contained in F.S. Regs., Part II. and the Staff Manual respectively. Title pages will be prepared in manuscript.

Place	Date	Hour	Summary of Events and Information	Remarks and references to Appendices
Outpost Duty	1917 April 9		A quiet day. At night the Batt was relieved by the 7th Gloucesters & marched back to billets in VILLERS-FAUCON. At the Batt was arriving at this village a big explosion occurred in a cellar & 6 men of the M.G. Coy were killed	
VILLERS-FAUCON	10		The day was spent in improving the billets & moving the men from cellars which German prisoners, w/h R.E. officer examined the cellars during the day for traps	
	11		At night, and on a very heavy snowstorm, the Batt took over the Outpost Line from 1/5 Gloucester Dispositions — B.H.Q in a trench at F 21 c 24 A Coy in reserve in BOULEAUX WOOD B – Support at F 21 c 24 C – on Left Front D – on Right Front	
	12		During the night A Coy moved to the Quarry in F 26 d 27. On our Right were the 4/5 Lincolns & on our Left the 1/6 Gloucester. Operation Orders received. The 144 Bde & the Bays on Left & Right to attack on the morning of the 13th inst at 4 a.m. the ridge from TOMBOIS FARM to MALAKOFF FARM. This Batt to attack the ridge from F 29 b 55 to F 23 b 96.	

A5834 Wt. W4973/M687 750,000 8/16 D.D. & L. Ltd. Forms/C.2118/13.

Headquarters
144 Infy Bde   TK 54

In reply to CM 201

Herewith a/c of the affair of
13.4.17 also of 1.4.17 -
The latter was done & the
former nearly done before your
note was received.

         F H Tomkinson
         Lieut Col Comdg
       1/1 Herts Regt

Attached are a few notes
as to points you ask —

         FHT

15/4/17

TK 55

Headquarters 144 Infy Bde
In reply to Cy 201

1. Section commanders had opportunities and seized them.
2. A post on the forward slope was found untenable & withdrawn.
3. L.G's by reason of their great mobility & firepower were of the greatest value.
4. When the position was taken the troops were too thick: thinning out was not easy on a/c of the shelling. If we had known the ground better we could possibly have thinned out before daylight.
5. Enemy morale very bad: half a Coy of determined men with 3 M.G's might have held up a Brigade as they had quite a good wire obstacle & it was almost as light as day. The attack was discovered at Zero – 21 minutes.

J. Tomkinson
Lt.Col. Cmdg
1/7 Bn The Worcs Regt

Operations of 1/7 The Worcestershire Reg^t on 13 April 1917.

On the night of 11/12th April the Battⁿ took over from the 1/8th The Worcestershire Reg^t the outpost line as shown on Map I.
The relief took place during & after a heavy snowstorm. There was very little accommodation & in most cases the men had to find their own shelter & dig themselves in.
C Coy. took over the Left front, D Coy the Right front, B Coy was in Reserve & A in Support.
The Battⁿ H.Q used by the 1/8 Worcs. Reg^t was found to be too far back & a fresh one made near the Support Coy in a bank at F 21 C 2 4.
During the night A Coy. was moved from BOULEAUX WOOD & to the Quarry near the Cemetery in F 26 d 2 7.
On the Right the line was held by the 2/5 Lincolns of the 59th Divⁿ, on our Left were the 1/4 Glosters.

At noon on 12th inst. orders were received from Brigade to attack on the morning of the 13th inst the ridge from approx F 29 b 8 5 to F 23 d 9 5. The attack being in conjunction with the 4th Glosters & the B^{des} on right & left, the objective of the operations being the TOMBOIS FARM — MALAKOFF FARM ridge.

A message was sent to warn Companies at 1.15 p.m & operation orders followed shortly after, a copy of which follows :—

Copy

Operation Order No 2 by Lt Col F M Tomkinson DSO commanding
1/8 The Worcestershire Regt.

Copy No 1.   12.4.17

Ref: 62 C NE 1/20,000

1. The Bde in conjunction with Bdes on right & left will advance the outpost line tonight.

2. The 144 Bde attack will be carried out by 7 Worcs on the Right & 4 Gloucesters on the left.

3. The 7 Worcs will attack from X Roads F29 central to QUEUCHETTES WOOD inclusive.
   A Coy will be on the Right & B Coy on the Left. Dividing line between Coys will be a line drawn East & West through F23c26
   The objective is the ridge running North from about F29 b 85 to F23 b 96.

4. For the purpose of the operations C Coy. 7 Worcs will be relieved by a Coy. of 4 Glosters by 11 p.m under separate arrangements.
   On relief C Coy platoons will report to the Adjt at Bn. H.Q.
   D Coy will remain in the line : O/C D will arrange to have thinned his line 1 hour before Zero time by withdrawing 1 Platoon to about F28 c 4.7 and one Platoon to F28 c 7.6.
   ~~D Coy will remain in the line O/C D~~
   D Coy will be in support and C Coy in Reserve, both under the orders of the C.O

5. Each Coy. will attack on a 2 platoon front with each platoon in 2 lines. Wide extending to be maintained & distances between lines not to be less than 200x.

6. Artillery arrangements will be notified later.

3.

7. O/C D will arrange with O/C A & O/C C will arrange with O/C B to make up to tools in A & B each to 50 shovels & 15 picks. Aeroplane flares, very lights, & SOS signals will be carried by A & B.

8. O/C C Coy will arrange to dump at the S. end of QUEUCHETTES WOOD by 12 midnight the 5 boxes of S.A.A. now with them & a further 3 boxes which C Coy will draw from B.H.Qrs. O/C C Coy will also establish & dig in a small post at this point by midnight. O/C D Coy will arrange to dump at X roads in F.29 a & b central by 12 midnight the 5 boxes SAA now with them & a further 3 boxes which D Coy will draw from B.H.Qrs.

9. Regimental Aid Post will be established NW of TOINE WOOD in Sunken Road at F.28 a 4.9.

10. A & B Coys will each carry 3 doz. mills grenades distributed singly.

11. Zero hour will be notified later probably 4 a.m. 13.4.17

12. O/C A & B will arrange to give their Coys hot tea before moving off. At 30 minutes before Zero hour A & B will be in position with their leading lines on the line from which they are to attack.
At the same time D Coy. will stand to in their positions & C Coy will stand to at present Bn HQ.

13. Rations for A & D for consumption on 13th will be taken to A Coys cooker tonight & rations for B & C to B Coys cooker. Companies must make their own arrangements for delivery & issue to the men.

14. All Officers taking part in the attack will carry rifles. A & B will dump Great Coats at their cookers before moving off.

4.

15. Advanced Bn HQ & signalling arrangements will be notified later.

16. ACKNOWLEDGE.

(Signed) R.W. Neeld
Capt.
Adjt 1/7 Bat. The Worcestershire Regt.

Copy No 1. retained
 No 2. 144 Bde for information
 No 3. 4 Glosters for information
 Nos 4,5,6,7 O/c Coys A B C D
 No. 8. Right Bn for information

Further operation orders were sent to O/c Coys at 5.15 p.m., reading as follows:—

Copy T.K. 34   12.4.17

Refce O.O No 2 paras 6, 11, & 15:—

Artillery Arrangements.

Field Artillery to fire along trench F.17.b.4.0 to F.29.b.9.5 during day. At dark to continue with occasional shots to stop work till 3.30 a.m.
Special shots bombarded F.23.b.9.5 & F.29.b.9.9.
Zero will be at 4 a.m on 13th inst. at which time the infantry will enter the enemy trench.
S.O.S signal will be sent up by order of O/c Coy if fire is wanted after 3.30 a.m.
Until 4 a.m any such fire will be directed on the enemy trench. After that hour sweeping fire on the two spurs 400x behind the objective. Five minutes fire will be given for each S.O.S sent up

Advanced Bn HQ & O.P. will open at Quarry at F 27 c 9 7. at 2.30 p.m

There will be a telephone station there & it is hoped to lay a line to F 23 c 4 4

ACKNOWLEDGE.

5.15 p.m.   (Signed)   J. M. Tomkinson
                                                Lt. Col.

At 5.30 p.m. a message was sent to the 2/5 Lincolns (the Battn on our Right) enquiring into their intentions on the morning of the attack, & enclosing a copy of our Operation Orders.

In reply a message was received stating that no special operations were to be carried out & that their attack on MALAKOFF FARM was not coming off.

This message was rather a surprise. The position of this Battn on our Right seemed very obscure & their intention not to advance was very upsetting as it meant that our Right Flank, if it took its objective, would be ~~in the air~~ Exposed.

The weather was now getting very bad. A heavy fall of snow looked like making the attack very difficult.

The snow continued until late in the night & remained on the ground during the advance, making men visible at a great distance.

Perceiving that danger was very likely to come to our Right Coy on account of the 2/5 Lincolns not moving, the C.O at 7. p.m sent a message to Brigade asking for howitzer fire on MALAKOFF FARM at 4 a.m & any other steps which might occupy the attention of the enemy there.

At 10.30 p.m the following order was given to O/c C Coy.
"Refer O.O No 2 para 12:—

At 2 a.m you will have your Coy. distributed as follows:—
(a) 1 Platoon (either 9 or 12) at F 28 a 4 7 under the orders of O/c D Coy
(b) 1 Platoon at about F 27 c 7 4 where B. Coy now have a platoon.
(c) 2 Platoons & Coy H Q at present B.H.Q.

At 3.30 a.m the Coy will be standing to as ordered in Para 12 O.O.2 but in the places indicated above."

As the night grew on the snow ceased & the sky cleared & at the time for getting into position the visibility was good, making it difficult to advance without been seen long before the objective was reached.

The preparatory stages were carried out with difficulty because so few of the troops knew the ground. Except for one section who lost their way, all were in position at the correct time.

At 3.39 a.m the enemy first detected something wrong & sent up many lights. This is not to be wondered at, for our men were plainly visible at several hundred yards on the snow.

At 3.41 a.m red lights were sent up & at 3.45 a.m Rifle & M.G fire was opened on our troops

At 3.54 a.m the Germans put down a fairly heavy barrage of 77 mm on the line of our forward posts last night. This quietened down about 4.2 a.m

By 4.4 a.m the enemy very lights appeared to come from much further East.

About this time the neighbourhood of Bn H Q in F 27 a was shelled with 4.2's & one of the cooks, 7th MATTHEWS, of B Coy, wounded fatally.

At 6 a.m messages were received from the attacking Coys:—

Lt. CARTER reported that A Coy was on the Right of the objective. He reported one machine gun & one prisoner taken & certainly three dead. Also that his left was held up first of all but had pushed forward again working rather too much to the right.

Capt. PRESCOTT reported that the objective had been reached with two Platoons, & without many casualties. He had not at that time got into touch with A Coy on his right half Coy. He reported that the trench was very shallow, but that the men were digging themselves in & improving their positions.

News was also gathered from other sources & it appeared that two other prisoners had been captured & evacuated through the 1st Gloucesters.

It was also reported that the enemy was in considerable strength, & that about 4 a.m he was either relieving or that some supports were coming up, for at that time from 45–50 Germans were seen advancing on our Right. A Lewis Gun was brought to bear on them & scattered them killing a good many.

At 6.10 a m a message giving this information was sent to Brigade.

At 7 p a m a message was received from Capt Prescott stating that it appeared to him that A Coy. were retiring & that a rumour had come to him that they (A Coy.) had been counter attacked & driven back.

2nd Lt. LITTLE also reported that he had seen considerable movement on the Right.

The situation on the Right seemed very obscure, until:—

At 8.10 a.m. a message from Lt. CARTER was received which read as follows:—
"My left post has been bombed & there are Boche attempting to outflank us there. My Lewis Gun has so far kept them back. I have fetched up 2,000 rounds of SAA & am keeping my support platoon up here until the left flank clears. We have been very accurately shelled & one of my L.Gs has been destroyed."

Shortly after this Capt. PRESCOTT reported his dispositions as follows:—

Three Platoons on line of road from about F23d93 – F23b98
One Platoon & Coy HQ at F23 a 85.

He also reported that he was in touch with A Coy & also 4th Gloucesters. Opposite our Left the enemy made away with a Machine Gun
During the morning the C.O. went forward to view the situation & on his return sent the following message to Brigade:—

Copy

H.Q
144 Infy Bde   13.4.17

I have been to F28 d 02 & F 29 b 98 to view the situation
The Battn is established along the following line:—
F28 d 10 – X roads F29 a & b central with L.G. post at F 29 b 30 –
X roads F29 b 98 – F 23 b 95.
I am in touch with 4 Gloucesters on my left & 59 Divn on my right
F29 a & b have been steadily shelled all day & at times heavily.
The enemy barrage after our attack was heavy across 29 a & 23 d
The 59 Div. inform me that enemy patrols frequently enter HARGICOURT.
I am gradually thinning my line, but this is made difficult by

the shelling.
I shall be relieved by 1/4 Ox & Bucks & shall hand over the following dispositions to their 3 Coys who relieve my 4 Coys tonight.
Bn H.Q. & Reserve Coy. as at present.
No 1 Outpost Coy from F28 d 02 to X roads F29 b 98 exclusive – 2 Pgts & 2 supports – Cy H Q TOINE WOOD.
No 2 Outpost Coy. X roads F29 b 98 inclusive to F23 b 95 – 2 Pgts & 2 supports. Cy. H.Q QUEUCHETTES WOOD.
We have captured 2 M. Guns & 5 Prisoners. Estimated number of killed varies from 12 to 50.
Our casualties are estimated at 6 killed 30 wounded.
4·2 how shells are falling steadily in Northernmost parts of F21 c.

Signed
F.M. Tomkinson
1 p.m   Lt Col. y Worcs.

The afternoon passed without special incident. The enemy artillery at intervals shelled the region of the RAPARIE in F21 c with 4·2 hows, & intermittently troubled our Right.

At 5 p.m Capt. PRESCOTT reported that our Field guns were firing on our own positions on the Left. This was immediately reported & stopped.

About 8·30 pm in the failing light the enemy evidently expected a continuation of our attack, especially on the Right. He put up a heavy barrage in front of TOINE WOOD from roughly F28 b N.E to F28 d S.W. This however did no damage & was too early to affect our relief.

The 4th Ox & Bucks began the relief at 8.25 p.m. The night was fine, but very dark. Our guides worked very well indeed & a successful relief was made.
The relief was complete at 12.30 a.m & the Coys. marched back when freed to a camp on the Railway at K 5 b.

F.N. Winkworth
Lt Col (md)
1/7 Bn The Worcestershire Regt

15/4/17

8th Worcs

Operations of 1/7 Bn The Worcestershire Regt against
GUILLEMONT FARM
on 24/25th April 1917.

On 23rd April orders were received that the Battn was, on the following day, to place two companies at the disposal of OC 8th Worcs Regt during their attack on GUILLEMONT FARM & the high ground in A.29.d. The Battn was at the time, holding the line. C Coy holding the Left Front, D Coy the Right Front, A Coy being in Support & B Coy in Reserve.

In the evening the 8 Worcs took over the line from us & we left A & B Coys in the Sector & at their disposal. Bn HQ & C & D Coys moved to a camp at F.25.a.8.6. being all in about 1 A.M, with orders to be ready to move at short notice any time after 3 A.M.

Zero for 8 Worcs attack was 3.45 A.M.

The Battn then awaited developments. At 7 A.M. news was received that the contact aeroplane had observed the 8th Worcs. digging in forward & had evidently got their objective.

At 8.15 C & D received orders to stand down. No more news was heard until a message came about midday to say that shortly before 9 A.M. the 8 Worcs had been heavily counter-attacked. The enemy advancing up the valleys on either side of the FARM had forced the Battn back to their former positions.

From information gathered later, it was heard that the platoon of A Coy under the command of 2nd Lt BUNDY had done very gallant work during the operations. These men took ammunition forward to the attacking forces right through the enemy barrage to positions close to the FARM. They were relieved at about 5.30 a.m.

to carry 8 boxes Lewis Gun pans & 12 boxes Bombs to GILLEMONT FARM from QUEUCHETTES WOOD. They were given 2 guides from B Coy.
There was much rifle, M.G. & shell fire at the time.

On reaching the trench on the high ground in F17d, it was found necessary to crawl in order to reach the road in F18c. Here they came under M.G. fire from both flanks & also from F24c - 1.2 practically in rear. By dint of rushing & crawling they reached a slightly sunken portion of the road in F13b ~~where they lied~~ about 100 yds from the Farm. From here to the Farm the road was so open that it was practically impassable. Nevertheless the three leading men — L/Cpl MARCHANT & Ptes COGGS & WILLIAMS — crossed the distance & delivered 3 boxes of pans to a Lewis Gun post at the S.E. corner of the Farm. These men afterwards rejoined the Platoon, Pte WILLIAMS being wounded.

L/Cpl MARCHANT again went to the FARM with a message pointing out the difficulties of the situation, & returned with orders to dump the remainder at about F13b32.

Four men were now wounded, one being a stretcher case. With this last, 2nd Lt BUNDY & a few men remained, whilst the Platoon was sent back.

Later the wounded man having been placed on a stretcher & started towards the Trench, 2/Lt BUNDY left Sgt OAKLEY (afterwards wounded) & followed his Platoon.

L/Cpl MARCHANT returned to Coy. H.Q., from where he guided some Stretcher Bearers forward, intending to return to the FARM, however he met the wounded coming back, which was fortunate as the Farm was by this time once more in the hands of the enemy.

The Platoon was caught in the very severe German barrage on the way back.

3

outline of

At 1.30 p.m the C.O was summoned to Brigade HQ & received orders to repeat the attack on the Farm at 11 P.M the same night with the 4 Glosters attacking on the Left & the 4 Ryl Berks on the Right

The Battⁿ at the time was very scattered for tactical reasons, & short time was available to make the necessary arrangements.

Major Parkinson, comm^g 4 Glosters was killed by a shell about 1 p.m which made things very awkward for the 4 Glosters.

Battⁿ H.Q was moved for the time being to the old position at F.21.c.3.4, & the C.O & B.C. & D Coy Cmd^{rs} went to H.Q 8 Worcs. to learn the latest news, & O.C Coys were then sent to reconnoitre the lines of approach, which as the ground on the Left was new to the Battⁿ, might present great difficulty.

The C.O also explained the general lines of the proposed operation.

Meanwhile Major ADSHEAD made the necessary arrangements for collecting B.C & D Coys at the Quarry at 7 p.m.

~~Orders were issued that the iron rations on the man will~~
~~Brigade Orders as follows were received at 7 p.m:—~~
~~be consumed: as this appeared rather scanty, biscuits~~
~~& bully, out of the ordinary ration were also brought~~
~~up & distributed. Ground sheets, packs & greatcoats were~~
~~dumped~~

Brigade orders as follows were received at 7 p.m:—

Copy.   144 Inf. Brigade Order No 174.
Ref Maps 1/20,000
62 C NE & 62 S NW   24/4/17

1/ The Brigade will continue tonight, the operations started this morning in conjunction with 126th Inf Bde., who will attack THE KNOLL from W to NW in conjunction with 4 Glosters.

2/ The attack will be carried out by 4 Glosters on Left – 7th Worcs in Centre – & 4 R. Berks on Right.

3/ 4 Glosters will attack the KNOLL from the South & South-West with 2 Coys. A third Coy will advance & dig in on the Southern slopes of the KNOLL to join up with 7th Worcs on their Right.

7 Worcs will attack GILLEMONT Fm from the S, S.W, W, & N.W with 3 Coys. The Right flank Coy will be responsible for gaining touch across the valley with the 4 Ryl. Berks.

4 Ryl Berks will attack COPSE in A 19 d & will be responsible for joining up to 7th Worcs & making the Right Flank secure by joining up to X roads in F 29 b 99.

The 4 Glosters & 7 Worcs will each have 1 Coy in Bn Reserve & the 4 Ryl Berks 2 Platoons in our present front line.

3/ 6th Glosters will be disposed as follows, after 4th Glosters come up :- 2 Coys in Ste EMILIE & 2 Coys in LEMPIRE, finding posts in present front line from TOMBOIS Farm inclusive to connect with Bnde. on our Left. HQ at Workhouse.

4/ 8 Worcs after relief by 7 Worcs will be disposed :- 2 Coys F 25 a 8 6, 1 Coy holding present front line from present Right to X roads in F 29 b 99, 1 Coy about F 22 b & d. H.Q. F 21 c 23.

4. Advanced Bde HQ will open at F 10 c 4 5 at 10.45 p.m.

5. 144 M.G Coy will have 4 guns in Brown line, 4 in present front system, & 8 ready to go forward to enfilade valleys & protect spurs after capture

6) O/C Cyclists will detail 4 Orderlies to report to Bde. Adv. H.Q. & 4 to report to O.C. 4 R Berks at Sunk Road F.23.c.53 at 10 p.m. & to await arrival.

7) Close touch must be obtained between Brigades & Battalions before Zero to prevent men of different units mistaking each other for the enemy.

8) The ground immediately West of GILLEMONT FARM was heavily barraged today by enemy & should therefore be avoided as far as is possible.

9) The C.R.E. will detail a strong party of R.E. & Pioneers to aid in consolidation — both Bde objectives — & a strong party of Pioneers to make strong points to cover both flanks of GILLEMONT FARM & the valleys lying North & South of the Farm.

Units will also consolidate as quickly as possible, paying special attention to the valleys & flanks of Spurs.

O/C Reserve Coys of units will be responsible for sending forward the working parties as soon as the situation permits.

10. At Zero the Artillery will open intense barrage on the objectives At Zero plus 10 the barrage will lift & the Infantry will enter the German Trenches.

11. Zero will be at 11 p.m.
Watches will be synchronised from the Brigade.

(Signed) J.N.S. Williams
Major
for Brigade Major
144th Inf't Bde.

Issued by signals at 6.20 p.m.

The following Operation Orders were immediately issued by the C.O.

Copy.

O.O. No 3 by Lt Col F.M Tomkinson DSO
Comm'g 1/7 Bn The Worcestershire Regt.

24.4.17

1. The Bn will attack & capture the German positions N.W & S of GILLEMONT FARM & will clear the FARM & the Eastern edge thereof.

2. C. Coy will be the Right, D the Left. B Coy in Support, A in Bn Reserve. C & D will each move in 2 waves each of 2 lines. B Coy will move in 1 wave of 2 lines. 30ˣ between lines, 50ˣ between waves. Objective will be A.7 South Sq. 07 to a line 50 yds N of GILLEMONT Fm. to a line 50 yds E of GILLEMONT FARM to A.13 South Sq. 6.5. Dividing line between front Coys the RONSSOY–GILLEMONT Fm. road inclusive to Right Coy. B Coy. will cover the whole front.

In rear of last line of C Coy. & of D Coy will move ½ a platoon 5 Ryl. Sussex to assist in consolidation.

In rear of the half platoon of 5 Ryl. Sussex with D Coy. will move 1 section R.E. They will construct a strong point for 12 men at F.12 South Sq. 9.5.

3. By 10 p.m O.c A Coy 7 Worcs will have his Coy. disposed as follows:—
   2 Platoons at QUEUCHETTES WOOD
   1 Platoon Sunken Rd. F.23.c.4.4
   1 Platoon Sunken Rd. F.17.a.3.4.

4. B.S.O. will establish telephone stations at F.24 Nth. Sq. 5.8, F.17.d.7.5, at QUEUCHETTES WOOD, & at Bn H.Q. And a reading station at about F.15.d.8.8. Assaulting Coys will endeavour to establish visual communication from GILLEMONT FARM.

5. Simultaneously 4 Glosters are attacking the KNOLL 140 Contours in F.6 & 12 and A.1 & 7. Also 4 Ryl. Berks are attacking the COPSE in South Square of A.19. C Coy are responsible for gaining touch across valley with 4 Royal Berks

6. Rations   Only Iron Rations to be carried. Great Coats & Ground Sheets to be left behind.

7. 80 Shovels & 10 picks per Coy will be issued to B C & D & an extra bandolier per man.

8. Bn H.Q will be at F.23 c.35, Aid Post at F.16 c.4.6, S.A.A. dumps F.24 a.07, F.17b central, & QUEUCHETTES WOOD

9. Ground immediately west of GILLEMONT FARM was heavily barraged by the enemy today, & will be avoided.

10. In consolidating, particular attention will be paid to valleys & flanks of spurs.

11. At Zero our Artillery will open intense barrage on the Objectives. At Zero plus 10 the barrage will lift & our infantry will enter the German position.

12. Zero hour will be at 11 p.m at which time the assaulting Coys will advance from the present used line.

13. ACKNOWLEDGE

Copy no 1 retained
2/3/4/5 Distributed to O.C. Coys 7.20 pm
6 to O.C. 4 Cheshires
7   4 Royal Berks   for information
8 144 Infy Bde

Signed
R W Nield
Capt & Adjt
1/5 The Cheshire Reg't

N ultimately transpired that at Zero -15 the 126 Infy Bde abandoned their operations & the 4th Royal Berks instead of capturing the copse in 19d & joining up with our left right were all back in our old front line by day break.

Between 7 p.m. & 8 p.m. B. C. & D. Coys. rendezvoused at the Quarry at about F 27 c 8.6. Here 80 shovels & 10 picks per Coy. were issued. Also 1 Mills Grenade & 1 extra bandolier per rifle.

Major Adshead carried through these arrangements & moved the Coys off correctly.

At 8.20 p.m. an alteration was made in No 2 of the B^{n} Operation Orders so as to conform to Bde Orders :—

The Ryl Sussex & the R.E. instead of going over with the infantry, were ordered to follow up later & were ordered to dig & wire a trench covering GILLEMONT FARM & 2 strong points in the valley South of the Farm. Other Pioneers were also given orders to make Strong Points at the head of the Valley N. of GILLEMONT FARM.

Brigade orders about this time were amended in that we had to take over the front line in our section of the attack: this was done very swiftly by Capt. WALLACE (O.C. A Coy) with 2 platoons. His remaining platoons at Zero hour were distributed, 1 in QUEUCHETTES WOOD & 1 near B^{n} H.Q.

At 2.20 minus 16 the assaulting troops of 4 Royal Berks were at my B^{n} H.Q. & it appears that they would be late.

The night was fine but very dark & no stars were showing when the time for getting into position drew near. The ground being only hurriedly reconnoitred just before dusk the same evening, the Company Com'rs had a very difficult job to get their men into position. This was however done to time & without incident.

The enemy had been very nervous during the early portion of the evening, but as Zero hour approached he became quite quiet & from 10 – 11 everything was quite normal.

Our troops advanced to time & the barrage put down by our guns was very strong. About 11.5 p.m double green lights, followed shortly after by single reds, were put up by the Germans & very quickly a heavy barrage of 77 m.m was put down a little behind our front line & from F.24.c.10 to about 6.29.a.25. 10.5 c.m guns also fired into the valley, but very few 15 c.m were noticed.

As our troops advanced, the Right Coy (C Coy) suffered a large number of casualties from our own Field Guns & their attack thereby was much disorganized. Part of the Company pushed forward under 2/Lt LEWIS & 2/Lt CAMPBELL & dug in North of the Road at about F.18.a.70, the remainder took up positions in the sunken road north of the barricade at about F.17.b.84 & in the trench running South of the Barricade.

2nd Lt LEWIS was killed early on by a bullet, & 2/Lt CAMPBELL had a nasty wound in his leg. This officer, however, bravely stuck to his post & refused to go back to the Aid Post until the afternoon of the 25th, when things were more settled.

D Coy were very successful in getting forward, thanks mainly to the skilful way in which the Coy Com'dr, Capt. G.G. WATSON got his men into position. Early in the advance this officer was severely wounded in the face & the work thereafter fell upon Lt LLOYD, who carried on as Coy. Commander in a very able manner.

10.

D Coy continued to advance & took up positions near the FARM without many casualties. A party under Sgt. DARBY formed a post on the Eastern side of the FARM at about A13 N3.8,6 & 2nd Lt. W.C. CASSELS & Lt. LLOYD dug in to the North of it.

At this time 2nd Lt. LITTLE engaged a party of Germans & killed three at short range with his rifle before been badly wounded in the hand by a bomb thrown by one of two opponents.

B Coy's left pushed on with D & formed posts north & north-west of the Farm under Lt. MELHUISH & 2nd Lt. BARTLETT

The right platoons of B Coy were held up at first 300-400 yds from their objective but were re-organised by Capt. PRESCOTT, & a post was formed at about A 13 N3 8y 34.

The posts now began to dig in hard & soon two lines of defence were formed & held during the night.

Before midnight Capt. PRESCOTT sustained a flesh wound in the left forearm & later on was knocked over by a low shell splinter hitting him on the back of the neck. He bravely stuck to his post & remained there until the Batt.n was relieved, being the last man of his Company into camp on the morning of the 26th.

About 4 a.m 2nd Lt. HIGGS-WALKER was sent forward with a party to carry S.A.A to the front posts. He did this successfully carrying forward 7000 rounds & on his return was able to furnish a very valuable report as to the situation.

At dawn there seemed considerable enemy activity on front & our posts were continually busy with Lewis Gun & Rifle fire. This continued until 6 a.m when the enemy made a determined counter-attack on the Farm & the flanks of it.

Heavy machine gun fire from a gun brought out of the Sunken road in A 14 c 8.9 & mounted on the high ground S.E of the FARM was formed on the Posts North of the FARM, especially on that held by Serg¹ DARBY. These posts now saw the enemy deploying to the attack from the BONY & MACQUINCOURT Farm roads & opened heavy fire upon them as they appeared over the ridge. The barrage, in answer to the S.O.S fell splendidly & did great damage. Our front posts now fell back deliberately to their second line of defence, which proved to be the old German trench in front of the Farm, & found it a strong position. The Lewis Guns & snipers did splendid work & the attack was broken up, the enemy retired into the sunken BONY Road & over the crest toward VENDHUILE, whilst a party seeking shelter in the FARM itself were caught by our Lewis Gun and rifle fire from Capt PRESCOTT's post East of the Farm & all wiped out, 20 bodies being counted. The forward posts were not again held, our men finding their second line a much stronger position.

This counter-attack was in strength, it is thought that at least 3 Companies were used. There is no doubt that the enemy was much shaken & lost a great many men. Many walked down into the barrage & the first 4·5" how. shell to fall was seen to fall into a bunch of six men, killing them all. The Lewis gunners worked splendidly & assisted greatly in stopping the advance. L/Cpl J.T. WILLIAMS, a sniper, was seen to kill 8 Germans on his own: this NCO also did good work later in patrolling & message carrying.

At 6·45 a.m. another counter-attack formed, but this was not on a large scale & was driven back by our men. The S.O.S was not sent up.

After this the situation became quiet & our stretcher-bearers did good work in getting in the wounded.

It was now ascertained that 2ⁿᵈ L¹ P.P. EDWARDS had been killed by a direct hit from a very heavy shell.

Whilst these things were going on the Pioneers & R.E. who had been unable to proceed to GILLEMONT FARM were kept in the old front trench at about E.17.d.8.3. They were here attached to O/c C Coy, to strengthen him & to improve his trench.

Also, in the early morning, the Bde. Cmdr. attached two Companies of 5 Glosters to the Battⁿ. Originally placed in the Sunken Road South of SART FARM, these men were gradually moved forward to take up positions in the Sunken Road north of the crossroads, in F.1.y.d.1 in QUEUCHETTES WOOD and see a reliable source.

Wounded were steadily evacuated all day, & by 4 p.m. all were got in that were possible in daylight.

All day our guns searched the hidden ground N.E. & E. of the Farm & sniped any Germans who showed themselves.

The Bony - GILLEMONT Farm Road was also frequently shelled to prevent troops being brought up hidden on the sunken portion.

During the afternoon the enemy was seen digging in about 300 yds. S.E. of the Farm & was shelled by the howitzers.

At 6 p.m. the number of wounded through the Reg¹ Aid Post amounted to 70 O.R, which included some 8th Worcs. wounded in the operations of the night 23/24 April.

In order to protect the infantry better in case of a counter attack, at the request of the C.O. who had consulted with the R.F.A, the barrage lines were shortened & now fell on the following Cmds:-

A.13.d.25 - A.14.a.0.1 - A.14.a.1.5 - A.7.d.9.1 - A.7.d.6.7

At dusk the forward posts pushed out small patrols from 60ˣ to 80ˣ according to the ground, paying particular attention to the flanks and in accordance with the Brigade Cmdrs personal orders to the Co.

During the day the position of the 4 Glosters on our left was very obscure & we could gain no information as to their true position.

At 8.40 pm a party of men were seen advancing quickly towards our Left Flank from the valley. It seemed certain that these men were Germans & some of our men fired. Luckily it was ascertained in good time that they were 1st Glosters, retiring on their former line. The enemy in front also appeared active in parts & a heavy hostile barrage came down. The situation seemed very obscure & the S.O.S. was sent up. Our barrage fell strongly on its arranged lines & quickly everything in front became quiet. The enemy at this time was very nervous & had evidently seen the Glosters on the move & our patrols advancing. It seems very uncertain that an actual attack was made, but whatever movement was going on in the enemy front was effectually stopped by the artillery.

During the relief no further counter attacks were made, on the other hand the enemy seemed to be very frightened that we should again attack him & on two other occasions he put up barrages which, however, did no damage.

After relief the Companies marched back to the Camp in K 5 central.

During the operations 1 Machine Gun & 1 Lewis Gun were captured, also a powerful electric signalling lamp.

The work of the artillery was magnificent. Certainly British shells did cause a number of casualties about the junction of F 17 d & F 18 c shortly after zero, but the remainder of the shelling was most effective & accurate. The barrages fell splendidly, & the careful searching of hidden ground beyond the Farm & the sniping of any germans who showed themselves, must have killed many Germans.

Since the operations many accounts of bravery & determination have been reported in addition to those mentioned above.
There is no doubt that the coolness & ability as leaders shown by Lt. A. LLOYD, 2/Lt J.W.D MELHUISH, & W.C. CASSELS determined the men to hold on to their positions & ~~hold~~ break up the strong counter-attack launched by the ~~enemy~~ enemy.
The Lewis Gunners all worked splendidly, but special note must be made of the ~~wonderful~~ excellent work of L/Cpl Q. SNEYD who did great work with his own gun, killing many Germans. Also under a heavy fire he righted another Lewis Gun which had gone wrong & brought it to bear on the German counter attack with decisive results.
Ptes J. PAYTON & A. BISHOP manned a gun, when all the team had become casualties, & although not knowing the workings of the gun very well, they opened a very effective fire, showing great courage & initiative.
Sgt H.S. HANDLEY & Cpl F. GREEN both did good work & showed great bravery & devotion to duty during heavy fighting.
Enough cannot be said of the stretcher bearers, especially Pte A. BREEZE who throughout the whole operation showed great bravery, getting away many wounded under heavy rifle & M.G. fire.
   Capt. W.R. PRESCOTT M.C. though shot through the arm early in the fight & later knocked down by a shell carried on in a most gallant manner & brought his Company into camp. He was evacuated to Hospital next day.
   Bn HQ does not appear to have been located by the enemy & only occasional shell fell around it.

No I.
Sketch Map showing dispositions immediately on
passing thro' village.

ETEHY.
QUARRY
LEVEL CROSSING
→ LEMPIRE
— A Coy.
— B Coy.

No II
Showing dispositions after consolidation
7-0 A.M.

D Coy

Army Form C. 2118.

WAR DIARY
or
INTELLIGENCE SUMMARY.
(Erase heading not required.)

Instructions regarding War Diaries and Intelligence Summaries are contained in F. S. Regs., Part II. and the Staff Manual respectively. Title pages will be prepared in manuscript.

Place	Date	Hour	Summary of Events and Information	Remarks and references to Appendices
	1916 Sept 27		On 25th the Batt. moved to a Camp in W Sector. Early calm by 2 a.m. The day was spent in resting & cleaning up	
	27		Working parties found at TEMPLEUX & FOSSE & FORBET. Remaining men in range	
			Working parties found by C & D Coys	
	28		The Batt. moved back to HANEL bivouacing along with 3rd Worcs	
	29		Moved Bivouac into Trench 187 H.Q. at 11 a.m. In the afternoon the Batt. moved forward to take over the Right Support positions from the 4 Rif Brigde. Dispositions :- B. Coy H.Q. at F.7.10.25 C & D Coy. at F.7.5.0 A Coy H.Q. 2 Platoons at TOWER WOOD. 1 & 2 Platoons in Quarry	
	30		Normal posture on the Brigade front. A quiet day. Oct 1st Relief commenced by a Battalion from the Tower Wood & Batt HdQrs	Total Casualties for the month Off Other Ranks Killed 3 37 Missing believed Killed 7 162 Wounded 1 11 Wounded Remained on Duty — 12 Missing — 9 TOTAL 9 330 Infantry Br Coy Lt Col W.H. WEBB Comdg 17th W Yorks R.

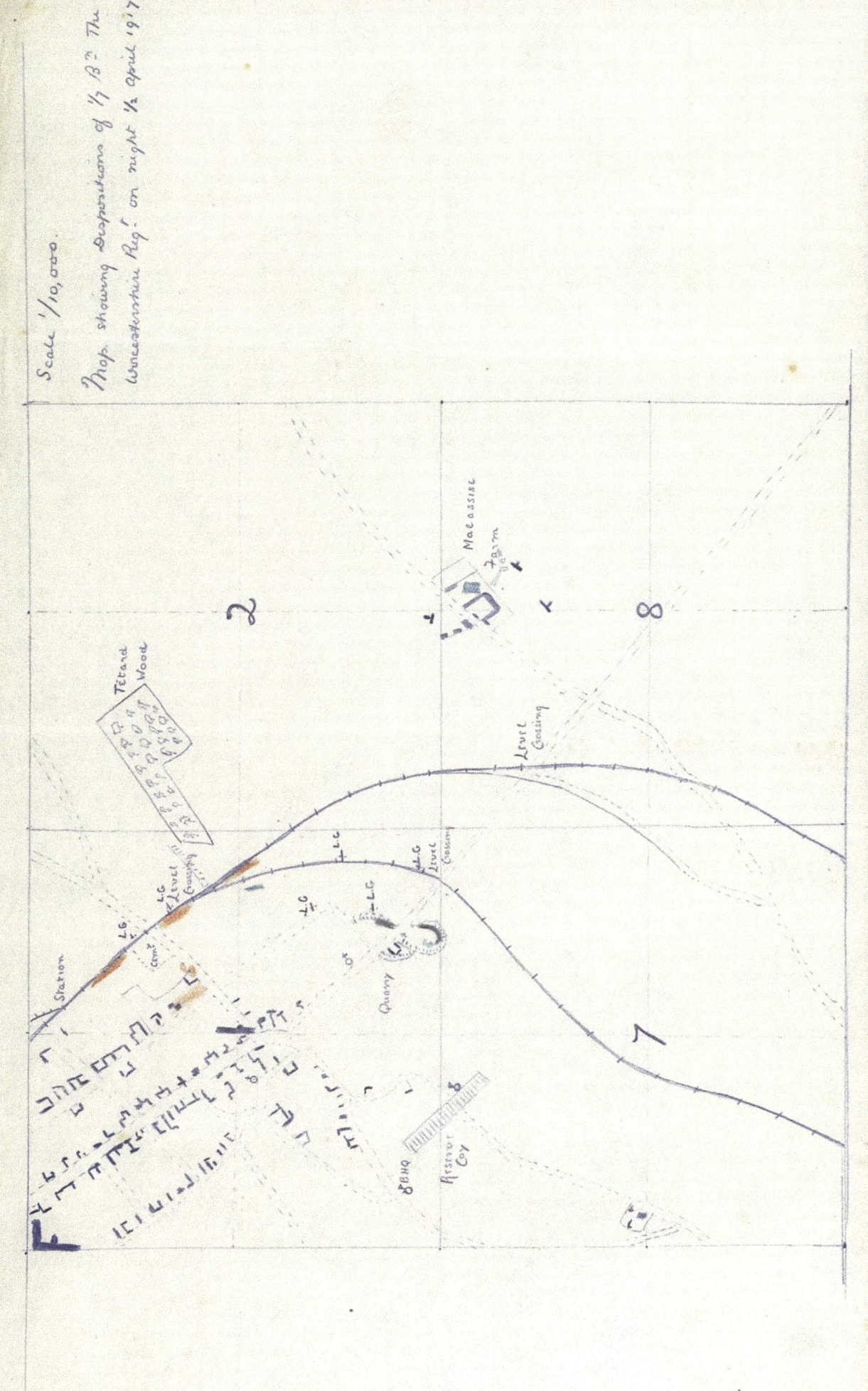

Confidential

Vol 27

Miss Thomas

M.27

1/4/28

War Diary of
the Worcestershire Regt.
1st May to 31st May 1917

(Vol. XXVI)

Army Form C. 2118.

WAR DIARY
or
INTELLIGENCE SUMMARY.
(Erase heading not required.)

Instructions regarding War Diaries and Intelligence Summaries are contained in F. S. Regs., Part II. and the Staff Manual respectively. Title pages will be prepared in manuscript.

Place	Date	Hour	Summary of Events and Information	Remarks and references to Appendices
Vignacourt	Nov. 1		In billets. Cooking parties on Peronne line relieved by 7 L.B. Lancs. Fus. 23rd N.Z. Bde. and marched back to HAMEL.	
HAMEL	2.		Cooking parties found as follows :– 1 Officer & 50 O.R. at TINCOURT 37 Ly on loading barges.	
	3.		1 Officer & 150 O.R. at ROISEL 67 Ly on loading ammunitions	
	4.		Remainder of Coys were & Rifles by the Armourer Sergeant. Coys placed at the disposal of B.O. Coys. for training.	
	5.		Captain & Adjutant M. Russell D.C.B. Coy. on training.	
	6.		2nd Lieut. Barrett gazetted Lieut. at his own Coy.	
			Coys. Commanded by his Majesty the King	
			"A" Coy — Capt. M. THATCHER.	
			"B" Coy — W. B. MARCHANT.	
	7.		Bn. moved to ROISEL to form advanced working party under the 5th Coy. R.E. "A" Remainder of M.G.B. under Coy. Commander to training for the attack.	
	8.		Coys at ROISEL. Remainder of Bn. in the shelters at his disposal of Coy Commander to training	
	9.		At ROISEL, Minerva by 1 Coy & 50 O.R. & Lewis Gun Cake at Tincourt attached to	
	10.		"A" Coy on Rifle Range in the afternoon 1 Coy + 50 O.R. & Cl.S. at ROISEL, also 1 Officer + 50 O.R. & Coy at work at 0/23 tunnel under No. 2 Rifle Coy. R.E. Remainder of M.B. English attack companies morning. In afternoon all the attack companies held by the aviation section Commander for instruction "Seem. Bombing Offrs.	
	11.		Brigade Bombing Offrs. Coys to a probable hour on the 13th inst., ret. all training Scarpe carries cancelled. Bln. & 20 min. 2 Coys attacked to M.K. (0) at ROISEL returned in afternoon to HAMEL.	
	12.		Orders to move to PERONNE recd. Bn. marched away at 6 p.m. to billets in FERMICOURT arrived at 2.30 p.m.	
PERONNE	13.		Bn. moved away at 5 a.m. and Lt. Warling sent away 49 QUINCONCE at 2 a.m. arrived in billets at 10.30 a.m. & marched out but returns ___ at corners 2 a.m. Lewis Gun.	

WAR DIARY or INTELLIGENCE SUMMARY

Army Form C. 2118.

(Erase heading not required.)

Place	Date	Hour	Summary of Events and Information	Remarks and references to Appendices
COMBLES	MAY 13		The Brigade was formed up just outside COMBLES & inspected by Corps Commander who presented medals.	
	14.		The Bde marched away on to the BAPAUME area, this Bn. having the starting point at 5.24 am.	
			A very cold day. 3 men fell out. The Bn. halted at BANCOURT at 9.15 am, & noted this amid snow & the NZA is MORCHIES into Divisional Reserve, taking up position from the outskirts of Lanes Pos.	
MORCHIES	15.		A quiet day. All Coys. at work at night making posts.	
	16.		Work on posts continued at night, rather dark with no attacks at 9 pm.	
	17.		A cleaner day. The village shelled a little in the evening.	
	18.		Quiet day. Working party 2 Officers 100 men & Officer 6/5 R. a Coy 1 Off. 100 OR. Bn. Coy. working on line 7.28.c. Houns of work. 9.15 pm – 2 am.	
	19.		Quiet day. Working party 2 Officers 100 OR. R. Coy. working on line 7.28.c. Houns of work as above —	
	20.		Village heavily shelled all day. 300 HE & 2 how. Took in village with occasional H.E. shrapnel. Bn. relieved the V/8 R. Warwick. Regt. in front line. Bn. H.Q. at I.14.6.9.2	
Front Line	22.		Army quiet day. Hostile aircraft very active.	
	23.		A patrol sent out at night from D.20 a 55 reconnoitred the ground in front of our right Coy, & did not trouble us.	

Army Form C. 2118.

WAR DIARY
or
INTELLIGENCE SUMMARY.
(Erase heading not required.)

Instructions regarding War Diaries and Intelligence Summaries are contained in F. S. Regs., Part II. and the Staff Manual respectively. Title pages will be prepared in manuscript.

Place	Date	Hour	Summary of Events and Information	Remarks and references to Appendices
Front line	23.		found no trace of enemy. Own piquets in D.20.b. Shelled lightly during the day.	
	24.		Against post out from D.20.b.91. much about 300 yds. in a N.W. direction. The enemy was sighted Sahil at a ranging about 500 yds. away were not engaged. This German Sahil was seen about of 30l 26 at D.22.c.95. Aiming party of small wiring party working in front of 30l 26 at D.22.c.95. 2/Lt Whorton + Pte Killa of Germans at LN.b.0. Pte Laker retired towards our lines. Pte Casualties 3 O.R. wounded.	
	25.		Visibility much impaired. Enemy was active in round Province during the day. Ashoma Sahil went out from 30l + 43 at D.20.a.53 at 11.45 p.m. under 2/Lt Bate. This patrol accounted a German listening post which ran both in owing our men. This post was alarmed + our patrol struck the disposition of 30l 31.45 p.m. and altered today. D.Coy was withdrawn from the Front line, these up the position of Right support. Blk remained fg from Coy. with a day till sunset. The usual working parties were sent out. This line from 30l 30. at about D.21.d.14. shot set out at 10.25 p.m.	
	26.		Ground in front was searched for bodies. No sign of enemy found. Enemy with very active shelling the battleries in rear with our directions. At 11 p.m. a fighting patrol under 2/Lt Foster was set from Pol 29 to search the road	

(6097). Wt W14299/M1393 75,000 1/17. D.D. & L. Ltd. Forms/C.2118/14.

WAR DIARY
or
INTELLIGENCE SUMMARY.
(Erase heading not required.)

Army Form C. 2118.

Place	Date	Hour	Summary of Events and Information	Remarks and references to Appendices
Bout/Vire	29		Morning. Though D.H.Q. Sherbot had Jyn about 150 x when it was suddenly heavily fired on from 2 ankos. positions about 50 x away. Two machine guns & a Lewis patrol were soon making in our DAHS to approach. The opening of fire was very sudden. They heavy Lewis patrol retired towards tk post. Post 29. Heavy fire on the enemy who had retired. Our casualties were 5. O.R. wounded & 4 O.R. missing. The Batt'n was in all probability wounded & taken prisoners. A patrol sent out immediately a.h. could find no trace of them.	
			Our scouts noticed an enemy batting of L & Jo firing during the morning at about 6.30 b. The artillery was informed & heavy guns brought to bear on the suspected spot. The batting was silenced & two large explosions heard. At midnight a fighting patrol of 1 O. & 2. Jr. with 2 Lewis guns left our post at about D.H. at 11. in the hopes of attacking an enemy post at D.30. a. 19. After ½ M. RATE advancing to D.30. a. 75. a small patrol of enemy 1800 was advancing. On being seen they were knelt down in the long Grass & our patrol forged on. The patrol then advanced but came under rifle & M.G. fire from front & right flank. This was also a risk or a pinch on the Rt. flank & was in danger of being taken. Our patrol returned. Rich Lewis target ammunition [?] & indication to have made good use of a clear target. Guns got into action claim to have made good use of a clear target.	

Army Form C. 2118.

WAR DIARY
or
INTELLIGENCE SUMMARY.
(Erase heading not required.)

Instructions regarding War Diaries and Intelligence Summaries are contained in F. S. Regs., Part II. and the Staff Manual respectively. Title pages will be prepared in manuscript.

Place	Date	Hour	Summary of Events and Information	Remarks and references to Appendices
Sun/ins.	29.		At night the Bn. was relieved by the 1/4 Warwick Regt. Relief was complete by 1.B. and the Bays. took up the positions on Divisional Reserve being in MORCHIES-BEAUMETZ line. 1000 Coys. in bivouac at BEUGNY. 1 B. H.Q.	
	30.		1 & 2 Coys. spent in ? marches. At night the Bn. was relieved by the 1/6 Gloucester Reg. + marched back to billets at FREMICOURT. 3 platoon Coys. + Bn. H.Q. in huts outside the village, one company in the village. 3.	⟨sig⟩
FREMICOURT.	31.		Day spent in rest & cleaning. Total Casualties for the month. Killed 25. Died of wounds 1. O.R. Missing ? 1 ? 13. O.R. Wounded 12. O.R.	

Comdg. 1/4 Bn. Warwickshire Regiment.

Confidential

Vol 28

Mr Brown 2.   M. 28

War Diary
of
the Worcestershire Regt. (T.F.)

for June to 30th June 1917.

(VOL. XXVII)

Army Form C. 2118.

WAR DIARY
or
~~INTELLIGENCE SUMMARY.~~

(Erase heading not required.)

Instructions regarding War Diaries and Intelligence Summaries are contained in F. S. Regs., Part II. and the Staff Manual respectively. Title pages will be prepared in manuscript.

Place	Date 1917 JUNE	Hour	Summary of Events and Information	Remarks and references to Appendices
FREMICOURT	1.		Day Spent in Training. A Coy. for inoculation	
do	2.		Divine Service. B Coy. furnish working-party of 1 Officer & 50 OR for Road Repairs.	
do	3.		Day Spent in Training. A Coy. for inoculation. 2 Casualties. H. OR. killed 10. OR. wounded. A Coy. by Shell 3.	
do	4.		do	
do	5.		do	
do	6.		Coys. placed at disposal of O.C. Coys.	
do	7.		The Battn relieved the 1/5 Bn R. Warwicks. Regt in Left Brigade Reserve. MORCHIES heavily shelled.	
Left Brigade Resv.	8.		A quiet day. Working Parties on mined dugouts. At night working parties on Posts near LOUVERVAL.	
do	9.		do Usual working parties found.	
do	10.		do	
do	11.		do	
do	12.		do	
do	13.		do	
do	14.		do	
BEUGNY + MORCHIES -BEAUMETZ Line.	15.		The Battn relieved by the 1/5 Bn R. Warwicks. Regt. Three Coys. go back to Camp at BEUGNY + one Coy. to the MORCHIES - BEAUMETZ Line.	
d	16.		Coys. at the disposal of O.C. Coys.	
do	17.		Divine Service.	

Army Form C. 2118.

WAR DIARY
or
INTELLIGENCE SUMMARY.
(Erase heading not required.)

Instructions regarding War Diaries and Intelligence Summaries are contained in F. S. Regs., Part II. and the Staff Manual respectively. Title pages will be prepared in manuscript.

Place	Date	Hour	Summary of Events and Information	Remarks and references to Appendices
BEUCNY & MORCHIES - BEAUMETZ Line	1917 JUNE 18.		Weather very hot. Coys. at Training during the day from 5.30 a.m. to 9.30 a.m. & from 6 p.m. to 8 p.m.	
do	19		do. 2 Coys. training from 6 a.m. to 8 a.m. 40 men on Working Parties from 8.30 p.m. to 5 a.m.	
do	20		do Coys. practice the Attack from 7 p.m. to 8.30 p.m.	
do	21.		3. Coys practice an attack on DELSAUX Farm.	
do	22		The Batt: relieved the 1/8 B: R Warwicks Regt as Left Front Batt: of Right Bde. Relief complete at 2.30 a.m. 23rd inst. Relieved by C. Coy. who had to wait until relieved in the MORCHIES - BEAUMETZ line.	
Left Front of Right Bde.	23.		A quiet day, no casualties. Working parties at night of front posts.	
	24.		do	
	25.		do	
	26.		do	
	27.		Front Posts & Tracks shelled at night. Two casualties. Both slight. Usual night working parties	

Army Form C. 2118.

WAR DIARY
or
INTELLIGENCE SUMMARY.
(Erase heading not required.)

Instructions regarding War Diaries and Intelligence Summaries are contained in F.S. Regs., Part II. and the Staff Manual respectively. Title pages will be prepared in manuscript.

Place	Date 1917	Hour	Summary of Events and Information	Remarks and references to Appendices
LEFT FRONT of RIGHT BDE	JUNE 28		Posts lightly shelled on Right during day, no casualties. Night very quiet.	
do	29		Right Coy HQ shelled in morning, no casualties. Night again quiet.	
do	30		A wet day. All quiet. Casualties for the month. Killed. 4. O.R. Died of wounds. 3. O.R. Wounded. 12. O.R.	

J.W. McKewan Lieut Col.
Commdg. 1/7th Bn. Worcestershire Regt.

Miss Brown 2

M.29

Confidential

Vol 29

War Diary
of
H.Q. &c. the Worcestershire Regt. (T.F.)

From 1st to 31st July 1917

(VOL. XXVIII)

Army Form C. 2118.

WAR DIARY
or
INTELLIGENCE SUMMARY.
(Erase heading not required.)

Instructions regarding War Diaries and Intelligence Summaries are contained in F. S. Regs., Part II. and the Staff Manual respectively. Title pages will be prepared in manuscript.

Place	Date	Hour	Summary of Events and Information	Remarks and references to Appendices
FREMICOURT	1917 July 1.		Relieved by 1st Bⁿ Royal Scots Fusiliers Relief Complete at 1.30 a.m. Battⁿ moved to the Army Camp at FREMICOURT. All in at 3.30 a.m.	
	2.		Battⁿ marched away at 2 p.m & arrived at ACHIET-LE-PETIT at 5.30 p.m. 1 man fell out	
	3.		March continued to BLAIRVILLE at 2 p.m. 2) OR fell out	
BLAIRVILLE	4.		Coys at disposal of O/C Coys for Section, platoon, & Coy Organisation & Inspection.	
	5.		Parades — 8-10 a.m. Section Training 6-8 p.m. Platoon Training. The C.O., S.M., Adj^t, & T.O. attend Divisional Tactical Exercise at BEINVILLERS.	
	6.		Parades as for 5th inst.	
	7.		Battⁿ paraded at 5.40 a.m & marched to BEINVILLERS, taking part in a Brigade Exercise. Returned to billets at 6.45 p.m.	
	8.		Sunday. Voluntary Church Service. No training.	
	9.		Route march & training in deployment. Distance 8 miles.	
	10.		Coys at disposal of O/C Coys for Section & platoon training	
	11.		Battⁿ Route March of 10 miles.	
	12.		Training of Sections & Platoons	
	13.		Route march of 10 miles	

Army Form C. 2118.

WAR DIARY
or
INTELLIGENCE SUMMARY.
(Erase heading not required.)

Instructions regarding War Diaries and Intelligence Summaries are contained in F.S. Regs., Part II. and the Staff Manual respectively. Title pages will be prepared in manuscript.

Place	Date	Hour	Summary of Events and Information	Remarks and references to Appendices
BLARVILLE	1917 July 14		Day spent on Field Firing Range	
	15		Brigade Horse Show	
	16		Batt. moved away at 4.40 a.m. & took part in Tactical Exercise near BIENVILLERS. Return 5 p.m.	
	17		Coys at disposal of O.C. Coys. for Platoon & Company Training	
	18		Route March. Distance 10 miles.	
	19		Coys at disposal of O.C. Coys. Exercise in Trench digging	
	20		March to BERLES-AU-BOIS at 5.30 p.m.	
BERLES -AU-BOIS	21		Coys at disposal of the Coys.	
	22		Entrain at SAULTY-LABRET at 8.59 for POPERINGHE area. Arrive in billets in POPERINGHE at 10 p.m.	
	23		Coys. at disposal of the Coys.	
POPERINGHE	24		6 a.m - 8 a.m Route march on pavé roads	
	25		Coys at disposal of the Coys.	
	26		6 a.m - 8 a.m Route march	

144/48

M-30

War Diary Vol 30
of
Worcestershire Regt T.F.

From 1/7/17 to 31/8/17

(Vol XXX)

WAR DIARY
or
INTELLIGENCE SUMMARY.

(Erase heading not required.)

Army Form C. 2118.

Instructions regarding War Diaries and Intelligence Summaries are contained in F.S. Regs., Part II. and the Staff Manual respectively. Title pages will be prepared in manuscript.

Place	Date	Hour	Summary of Events and Information	Remarks and references to Appendices
Camp A 2nd	Aug. 1		Coys wet no training possible	
do	2		do	
do	3		Coys at disposal of O.C. Coys for reconnaissance of O.G. 1 & 2 by Officers and N.C.O's	
do	4		do	
do	5		do	
do	6		Bn. moved to Camp at A 27 at 8.30 a.m. all in by 10.30 a.m. Distance 3 miles	
Camp at A27	7		Coys at the disposal of O.C. Coys for training	
do	8		Bn moved to Camp at A pm. A 20 c 71. all in at 4. P.M.	
Camp at A 30 c 71.	9		Coys at disposal of O.C. Coys for training	
do	10		Coys at disposal of O.C. Coys for training. Baths 8 A.M. - 10 A.M. 2nd Lieut H.T. Williams joined by jolling R.A. Staff.	
do	11		Coys route march 6000 yds	
do	12		Church Parade at 11 A.M. North Staff & R. Warwick Regt and 2nd Worcestershire Regt G.O.C. Division attended.	
do	13		Coys at disposal of O.C. Coys for training	
do	14		do	
do	15		Bn moved to REIGERSBORG CAMP at 1.15 P.M.	

WAR DIARY
or
INTELLIGENCE SUMMARY.
(Erase heading not required.)

Army Form C. 2118.

Place	Date	Hour	Summary of Events and Information	Remarks and references to Appendices
	Aug 16		The Bn. went forward in support to the leading Bn. of the Bde Reserve on our left. of the 145 Bde in attack on LANGEMARCK LINE Bn. HQ moved at 2.15 am to KULTUR FARM. D Coy moved at 4.15 am to REGINA CROSS and ALBERTA 100× W. of STEEN BEEK. "C" "B" and "A" Coys moved to O.G.1., O.G.2. and O.B.1. At 11 am orders were received to move the Bn forward over the STEENBEEK to fill a gap in the line said to exist between the left of our Bn and the right of the 11th Div. "D" Coy were ordered to cross the STEENBEEK C Coy to move to "D" Coys old position. "B" Coy to ALBERTA A Coy 200 yds W. of KITCHENERS WOOD. Bn. H.Q. moved to O.11.a.6.1. At 5.30 pm orders were received to capture MON DU HIBOU and TRIANGLE FARM. C Coy were detailed with ZERO at 7.30 PM. Attack was launched and men were going well when checked by MG and sniper and would not go further together. Capt. B. Montgomery and 2 Lieut. Haywood were wounded. 4 OR killed 37 OR wounded and 12 OR missing another attack on MON DU HIBOU orders were received to launch another attack on MON DU HIBOU which ZERO at 2.30 am. 17th "B" Coy were detailed to make the attack. Intense shelling all day	
	17	2.30 am	"B" Coy moved forward to the attack, reached their objective and commenced to consolidate when enemy counter attacked and drove them back about 150 yds where they dug in and held on Capt. Brown & 2nd Lieut. Beck were wounded 3 OR killed. 28 OR wounded 6 OR missing	

Army Form C. 2118.

WAR DIARY
or
INTELLIGENCE SUMMARY.
(Erase heading not required.)

Instructions regarding War Diaries and Intelligence Summaries are contained in F. S. Regs., Part II. and the Staff Manual respectively. Title pages will be prepared in manuscript.

Place	Date	Hour	Summary of Events and Information	Remarks and references to Appendices
	Aug. cont. 18.		C. Coy moved back to position vacated by "B" Coy on W. Bank of STEENBEEK. The Bn. was relieved by 2 Coys 1/8 Worcestershire Regt. Relief commenced at 9.30 P.M. and was complete at 12-10 A.M. Owing to the ordinary good relief when taking into consideration the amount of hostile shelling. The Bn. moved to CANAL BANK - all in at 2-45 A.M. The total casualties suffered during the past 48 hrs were as follows.	
			Officers O.R.	
			KILLED 18"	
			WOUNDED 6 95"	
			WOUNDED + remained at duty. 2 14	
			MISSING. nil 20	
Canal Bank	18		Bn. moved to REIGERSBURG CAMP. after arrs. Arr in by 6.10 P.M.	
REIGERSBURG CAMP	19		Day spent in inspections and cleaning.	
do	20		do	
do	21		"B" and "C" Coys move to Canal Bank after tea	
do	22		"B" and "C" Coys move from CANAL BANK to O.S.1 + O.S.2.	
do	23		"B" & "C" coys at O.S.1 + O.S.2.	
do	24		Bn. moved to Billets in CANAL BANK.	
CANAL BANK	25		Bn. took over the line from 4th Flintshire Regt. "B" Coy Left front and "C" Coy Right front. "B" Coy ALBERTA. "C" coy to O.S.1.	
			A Coy to 4 to ALBERTA. Bn. H.Q. to ALBERTA.	

WAR DIARY
or
INTELLIGENCE SUMMARY.
(Erase heading not required.)

Army Form C. 2118.

Place	Date	Hour	Summary of Events and Information	Remarks and references to Appendices
	Aug. 26		Bn ordered to take part in attack on LANGEMARCK G. LINE with 8th Wor on right and 32nd Bde. on left. A + D Coys moved to assembly trenches in front of MON. DU. HIBOU on night 26/27.	
	27		Bn attacked L. + G. line with ZERO hour at 1.55 P.M. and attacked in the following order A Coy + 2 platoons of B Coy under command of Capt. Wallace P.P.M.C. on right. D Coy and 2 platoons of B Coy under command of Capt. A.O. Lloyd on left. C Coy in Bn. reserve. Bn HQ. at MON.DU.HIBOU. Bn A-10 POST. at ALBERTA. Orders for relief by 145 Bde received at 11 P.M. Part of Bn coys relieved and marched back to DAMBRE CAMP. arriving during the morning. Capt. A.O. LLOYD, 2nd Lt BURKE 35 O.R. "D" Coy 30. O.R. B. Coy. 11. OR. "C" Coy. "A" Coy did not get relieved until night 28/29 and arrived in camp at 4 A.M. Casualties for action. KILLED WOUNDED MISSING. WOUNDED REMAINED ON DUTY.	OFFICERS. O.R. 1 21 4 68 nil 4 1 3 received by all ranks
DAMBRE CAMP.	28.		Day spent in rest which was badly needed by all ranks.	

WAR DIARY or INTELLIGENCE SUMMARY

Army Form C. 2118.

Place	Date	Hour	Summary of Events and Information	Remarks and references to Appendices
DAMBRE CAMP	Aug. 29		Bn. moved to SCHOOLS CAMP. arrived at 1.10. P.M.	
SCHOOLS CAMP	30		Coys at disposal of O.C.Coys for cleaning and interior economy	
do	31		Coys at disposal of O.C.Coys for training	

Casualties for the Month

	K in A	D of W	M	W	W & R	TOTAL
Officers	1	2	–	9	3	15
Other Ranks	38	2	14	181	19	254
	39	4	14	190	22	269

The following is a more detailed a/c of the operations of 16th–17th Aug. and 26th–28th Aug. 1917.

J.H.Tomkinson Lieut. Col.
Comdg. 17th Bn. Worcestershire Regt.

WAR DIARY
or
INTELLIGENCE SUMMARY.
(Erase heading not required.)

Army Form C. 2118.

Place	Date	Hour	Summary of Events and Information	Remarks and references to Appendices
			Operations of the 1/4th Battalion the Worcestershire Regiment. 16th - 17th August. 1917.	

ZERO for the attack by the 145th Infantry Brigade on the German position East of the STEENBEEK was at 4.45 am 16th. This Bn. was under orders to leave one Coy. on the STEENBEEK at ZERO plus 3 hours and the remaining Coys. in O.B.1. and O.B.1. by ZERO plus 5 hours.

At 4.30 A.M. Bn HQ moved to O.B.2. near CIVILIZATION FARM, "D" Coy moved E of HUGEL HALLER - + Bn. O.P. was established to the left of OBLONG FARM.

The remaining three Coys. crossed the canal at 6.45 A.M. and moved to positions as ordered.

We were not able to obtain any definite information either from Divisim or our own O.P. At 6.35. A.M. enemy barrage heavy on the STEENBEEK and KITCHENER'S WOOD LINE.

At 11 A.M. orders were received from Division to move the Bn. to a position of readiness E of the STEENBEEK because the left Division had reported that their right had lost direction, and was not in touch with our left

WAR DIARY
or
INTELLIGENCE SUMMARY.
(Erase heading not required.)

Army Form C. 2118.

Place	Date	Hour	Summary of Events and Information	Remarks and references to Appendices
			Still no definite news from the front.	
		11.30 am.	The Bn. commenced to move as follows:—	
			"D" Coy to E. of STEENBEEK & C.II.B.	
			"C" Coy Between the STEENBEEK and HUGEL HALLES	
			"B" Coy About ALBERTA	
			"A" Coy about CANOPUS. SUPPORT.	
			Bn. HQrs at— C.II.A.66 near REGINA CROSS.	
			From Reconnaissances particularly by Capt. Lloyd M.C. it appeared that the 145" Bde had made very little ground on our front; that they were barely held up in front of MON DU HIBOU and HILLOCK FARM, that they captured no part of the LANGEMARCK - GHELUVELT Line, and had except for some small isolated parts been driven back on the STEENBEEK when they held a very irregular line never more than two or three hundred yds. E. of the STEENBEEK. During the run up of the Bn. Shelling was very heavy, and remained very heavy for the next twelve hours particularly in the line REGINA CROSS to ALBERTA causes rifle fire from German posts also caused casualties. On the other hand our leading troops found a number of good rifle targets which they shot with to good effect. The general position was reported to Brigade by runner timed 1.45 P.M. At 4.15 orders were received from Brigade to reconnoitre with a view to attacking MON DU HIBOU at dusk.	

Instructions regarding War Diaries and Intelligence Summaries are contained in F. S. Regs., Part II. and the Staff Manual respectively. Title pages will be prepared in manuscript.

Army Form C. 2118.

WAR DIARY
or
INTELLIGENCE SUMMARY.
(Erase heading not required.)

Instructions regarding War Diaries and Intelligence Summaries are contained in F.S. Regs., Part II. and the Staff Manual respectively. Title pages will be prepared in manuscript.

Place	Date	Hour	Summary of Events and Information	Remarks and references to Appendices
			At 6.20 P.M. orders were received to capture strong post at TRIANGLE FARM, VANCOUVER and MON DU HIBOU without artillery preparation. A telephone message had been received at 5.15 P.M. forecasting this operation. At 6-7 P.M. O.C. 'C' Coy received his orders to carry this out that-time dug in on the W. bank of the STEENBEEK in 11B. Zero was 7.30 P.M. At ZERO "B" Coy were to move to W. bank of the STEENBEEK from ALBERTA and "A" Coy were to move to ALBERTA. At ZERO "C" Coy advanced to the attack. they immediately came under heavy machine gun and rifle fire from the German positions in their right and from MON. DU HIBOU. Their leading wave was nearly all wiped out. Capt. Montgomery was hit through the stomach, and Lieut. Haywood was shot through the knee. "D" Coy had endeavoured to provide covering fire with Lewis Guns but the rifle grd machine gun fire from the German positions on the right made this very difficult. 2nd Lieut. Sadut, situated by R.S.M. Mole took over the Coy, and dug in about 350 yds E. of the STEEN BEEK and facing MON. DU. HIBOU. A telephone message was received from Brigade about 11 P.M. and conformed by wire received at 1.20 A.M. to renew the attack with ZERO at 2.30 A.M. and with a standing barrage on the objective. For this operation "B" Coy was moved from the STEEN BEEK & "C" Coys position in front of MON. DU. HIBOU	

WAR DIARY
or
INTELLIGENCE SUMMARY.

Army Form C. 2118.

and the latter moved back to the STEENBEEK.
The attack was delivered with determination and despite casualties some of
our men reached part of the objective.
Him 2nd Lt H.B. BATES who had shown great courage and determination and
Capt. W.N.S. Brown were both badly wounded.
Parties of Germans appeared with bombs and our men were driven out and oku
in and then leaving line about 100 yds. S.W. of Mon O.U. 11200. About
then these position was taken who had probably had formed on of
the German front line.
2nd Lieut Hoover took over command of "B" coy and reorganised.
The evacuation of the wounded of "C" + "D" coys was extremely difficult, but
carried out with great gallantry by stretcher bearers and others.
Through the whole of the 17th the shelling was heavy and continuous and
caused many casualties. At the same time many Germans appeared to
be in a low state of morale and some made efforts to surrender to "B" Coy
which were not successful.
Communication was maintained with the Brigade throughout the whole
of the operation except for very short periods and for an advanced
in the evening of the 17th owing to firm went by Bn. and Bde. Signallers
At 9.30 P.M. the relief of the Bn. by two coys of the 8th Worcesters
commenced, meantime the scattered and disorganised troops of the 145 Bde.

Army Form C. 2118.

WAR DIARY
or
INTELLIGENCE SUMMARY.
(Erase heading not required.)

Instructions regarding War Diaries and Intelligence Summaries are contained in F. S. Regs., Part II. and the Staff Manual respectively. Title pages will be prepared in manuscript.

Place	Date	Hour	Summary of Events and Information	Remarks and references to Appendices
			whilst were on our front had been on juvenile withdrawn. Their troops had a very hard time having been heavily shelled and their formation broken up before ZERO for them without attacks. they have been unable to keep up with the artillery barrage, and had therefore been met with heavy machine gun and rifle fine. Their casualties however on our front was not much heavier than our own. The relief proceeded well and was complete about 11.15 P.M. The trench from ALBERTA to OBLONG FARM was heavily shelled during most of the relief and gas shells were encountered E. of the canal. The gas was worse than those at ALBERTA, there had not been available for us because 1/2 Cwt Such was there 2nd Lt. J.T. BURTON acted as liaison officer with the right Bn of the 11th Bde who were on our left, and 2/L Lt. H.W. Turnbull performed a similar duty with the 8th Quebec Regt. these officers were reported to have done under shell fire. The Regl medical Aid Post was at ALBERTA where Lieut Milligan the Bn M.O. did much good work. + Cap (Capt) R.R. Wallace M.C.) received the rations from OBLONG FARM and delivered them correct under great difficulties.	

WAR DIARY
or
INTELLIGENCE SUMMARY.
(Erase heading not required.)

Casualties

Officers:
Capt. A.R. Montgomery (since died) Capt W.N.S. Brown
2nd Lt. R.S Leuter. 2nd Lt. R.H. Hazlewood... 2nd Lt. H.B. Batt..
2nd Lt. W.J Flower (since) Capt. A. Lloyd M.C. and 2nd Lt. R.P. Thomas
were wounded and remained on duty

Other Ranks.

Killed — 21.
Wounded — 102
Wounded but remained on duty — 16
Missing — 12
                    ———
Total Other Ranks 151

The Bn moved to CANAL BANK after relief.

WAR DIARY or INTELLIGENCE SUMMARY

Army Form C. 2118.

Operations of the 1/7 Bn. The Worcestershire Regt.
26th and 28th August 1917

On the 22nd August the C.O. was informed that the 7th and 8th Bns would in the near future attack a portion of the LANGEMARCK–GHELUVELT line, and also take up our outpost position on the I.E. of such line running roughly from FLORA COTT to GENOA.

On the 23rd provisional orders were issued to O.C. Coys and the question of objectives discussed.

On the evening of the 24th the Bn. was concentrated in the CANAL BANK.

On the 25th A+D coys were moved up about 0.8.1 in relief of coys of 5th Worcesters and 4th Gloucesters. C Coy sent an attached coy of the 4th Worcesters moved up to the front line taking over from the 4th Gloucesters a line running roughly from C.6 central to Cam Rd C.6.5. to trench at C.12 b.18. having tried until the Warwick Rd at about C.12 a.24. and with the 11th Division at about C.6 central. "B" Coy moved to ALBERTA and was billeted in the BOND.

Bn HQ moved to ALBERTA in relief of 4th Gloucesters.

The relief was considerably interfered with by a hostile barrage on the ADMIRALS ROAD and the KITCH ENEERUn which caused 10 casualties. Relief was complete about 12.30 AM. The troops were carrying rations for consumption on the 26th, rations and water for consumption on the 27th were brought up and delivered to the forward coys by "B" Coy.

A supply of Auto Bourlands and an extra supply of rum were issued by Brigade and found most useful.

Previous to relief assembly trenches had been commenced about 15 of HILLOCK FARM - KIERSLARE ROAD, and the 477 Field Coy RE. were engaged in camouflaging same as advantaged.

The whole of D Coy from ALBERTA were employed in continuing the dugin of these trenches from midnight 25/26 to dawn 26th. About 8 PM on the 26th the Bde orders for the attack were received and subsequently a message notifying that ZERO would be 1-55 PM on the 27th.

Bn orders and instructions to accompany same were thereupon written and circulated to coys.

The objective after this Bn were roughly VANCOUVER, the LANGEMARCK - GAELUVELT line and a line of outpost 150 yds east thereof.

WAR DIARY
or
INTELLIGENCE SUMMARY.
(Erase heading not required.)

Army Form C. 2118.

Place	Date	Hour	Summary of Events and Information	Remarks and references to Appendices
			Capt. of A Battalion and Capt. Carter M.C. with reconnoitred the assembly trenches and developed on the allotment thereof. It was found necessary for our party moved to work on the 5 & 6 Worcester assembly trenches. The situation was between Bois ne very little a true line between Div 2 from VANCOUVER to 4th Worcesters, and the dividing line between Div 2 from VIEILLES MAISONS and FLORA COTT. to the 32nd Bde of the 11th Div. During the relief of the 4 & 5 Worcester a heavy bombardment started in the front of the Corps on the right, whereupon the Germans put up an S.O.S. on our front which brought down heavy artillery fire between our assembly trenches and the STEEN BEEK. At 2.20 A.M. orders were issued for the assembly. B Coy provided guides for this. The necessary improvements soon arose – was painted out. A report was sent to the Brigade and the assembly trenches. The day of the 26th was our personal quiet on our front. At 9.30 P.M. Bn HdQrs moved from ALBERTA to MON DU HIBOU This is a heavy cemented building containing an large room down stairs a cup-bn upstairs with 4 loop holes and a small room also on the ground floor adjoining the large room. Between the ground floor and the cupola is a layer of concrete about 4 feet 6 inches and in the roof there is about 2 ft [?]	

WAR DIARY
or INTELLIGENCE SUMMARY
(Erase heading not required.)

Army Form C. 2118.

Instructions regarding War Diaries and Intelligence Summaries are contained in F.S. Regs., Part II. and the Staff Manual respectively. Title pages will be prepared in manuscript.

Place	Date	Hour	Summary of Events and Information	Remarks and references to Appendices
			This extraordinary shelling by an even outnumbered force points to previous to 77 mm shell fire against 4.2" & 5.9" and perhaps on the foot. The objects were an open warfare and destroying in the certain ditch. The condition of the troops which endured many A & C coys from D.S.I were rendered very difficult by (1) intense darkness (2) heavy rain (3) great congestion in the trench, and (4) shelling which was at times heavy. However by 3 am the zero this was complete and reported to Bde. coy after dawn on the 27th Head quarters 1/8th Worcester moves from	
ALBERTA		TO MON DU H/1800	It arrived 16 of the troops remained behind from the enemy until ZERO. Time was length and due to the green camouflage went down by the R./E. and the patient waiting by the infantry. The morning was quiet mentally quiet between 12 noon & 1pm. About 12 noon rain fell. The remainder of the afternoon was very heavy. The progress of the artillery barrage in front of our present line was to be at the rate of 100 yds in 8 minutes. Eventually at 21:50 a very heavy barrage and bombardment was opened up by our artillery. It broke out the enemy trench and advanced full assault	

WAR DIARY
or
INTELLIGENCE SUMMARY.
(Erase heading not required.)

Army Form C. 2118.

Place	Date	Hour	Summary of Events and Information	Remarks and references to Appendices
			Capt. Wallace lived for about 1½ hours Sgt Newstart had & keep him at was to continue the battle. The Coy went on badly held up, they had rifle cover they could and engaged the enemy in a rifle fight. Very good results were obtained chiefly by men running to the wounded black Kaffirs there were very effective death until and 40-60 germans were killed. The left Coy Capt. A.O. Lloyd M.C. plus two Platoons started from B Coy advanced in the avenue the trenches and made good progress. He stormed in C.6.d central & then found to be very bad and the Coys were not able to link up with the company to the west of the city reached the line from about 26.d.65 - 26.C.b.67. Roughly about 60 got in front of the LANGIE MARSH - GHELUVELT line. He enemy also showed a disposition to surrender out they died not take place in our men were coming which having machine gun fire from the right which caused the men to shoot a number of germans in there front whom the remainder who intended to surrender helped an subsequent attack. The garrisons lived in LANGIE behind a hedge C6d31 & C6d67 & C6d80	

WAR DIARY
or
INTELLIGENCE SUMMARY.
(Erase heading not required.)

Army Form C. 2118.

Place	Date	Hour	Summary of Events and Information	Remarks and references to Appendices
			A german machine gun was firing from an open emplacement in the angle of the Lilly at c.6.d.55.75. Other MGs were also firing from enemy emplacements at approximately C.6.b.50 and C.6.d.6.8. VIEILLES MAISONS was also holding up the 11th Bn: who had not taken their point. The germans attempted to mount a machine gun at the side of the building at C.6.d.85 which appeared to be a strong point, but we killed the first ten men who appeared and they abandoned the attempt. The barrage having passed away our troops were now pinned down by rifle and machine gun fire from the front and flanks, but obtained many good targets to their left flank and some on their front. Some about 60 germans were assembled for Capt Hodges, who now moved up into the front line to ascertain the situation and was not able to get back. At dusk Capt Lloyd Jones, who had, on the air arm being unable to advance with their jobs and dug in while affecting this to received a rather changed his shoulders. C.S.M. Shakespeare showed great courage and determination though the fight.	

WAR DIARY
or
INTELLIGENCE SUMMARY

Army Form C. 2118.

(Erase heading not required.)

Place	Date	Hour	Summary of Events and Information	Remarks and references to Appendices
			The barrage was very heavy and very accurate, and any fire shells fell short. The infantry advanced in good order but the going was very difficult from the start. Many men found themselves stuck in the stiff toffee-like mud & their boots and kit were not quite fit enough to keep up with the barrage, although the troops turned up when about 50 yds off it. There was a big number of Germans in shell holes in our front, they at first showed an inclination to surrender, but when they saw the small difficulty we found in movement, they altered their tactics and as the barrage passed over them opened a heavy fire. The 149th Bgd. Capt. G.R. Wallace M.C. plus two platoons attacked from B Coy advanced beyond the place marked rendezvous on the map and captured a Gun about 100 yds N. Two enemy machine gun emplacements at approx. C.6.d.5.4. Unfortunately Capt Wallace who was leading his men in a very gallant and determined manner was hit in the stomach by one of his own snipers in his right front and fell to the ground. Sgt Matthew rushed to his assistance but was shot through the face. Sgt Handcock then assisted Capt Wallace and was stopped with fractured by a bullet about this time. Sgt Cooper Eden and Miller also were killed.	

WAR DIARY
or
INTELLIGENCE SUMMARY.
(Erase heading not required.)

Army Form C. 2118.

Place	Date	Hour	Summary of Events and Information	Remarks and references to Appendices

Very heavy rain set in and the consolidation of this position was found impossible. The troops were up to their waists in water.

Capt Lloyd therefore withdrew his Coy and consolidated a line in touch with the 11th Division at about C.6.d.49. At 4 P.M. 2nd Lt Banks took out a platoon of 'C' Coy (Bn Reserve) and closed a gap which had opened between A & D Coys.

The forward troops were not in front of my forward position but whilst in their forward position but at about 4P.M. in reply to our alarm sign. the enemy put down a very heavy barrage along the line from MON. OO. 41800 towards ST. JULIAN. Then while the 145 V Bde who had relieved the CANAL BANK at ZERO moved to STEENBEEK at about 5 P.M.

The intention had been that their Runners advance through our line in patrons further E. They did not however come up to a new our line. The H.Q. of the Coy Bricks and the Bricks Bn were in concrete dug outs about 100 yards E. of MON OO 41800. The C.O. of Blue Bn urged them to hasten the relief of our troops but they did not reserve orders.

WAR DIARY
or
INTELLIGENCE SUMMARY.
(Erase heading not required.)

Army Form C. 2118.

Place	Date	Hour	Summary of Events and Information	Remarks and references to Appendices

At 11.20 P.M. was received a wire stating that the relief had been ordered packed in own concealed to them. They thereupon effected a relief of a portion of our 'C' Coy which went to Bn reserve and portion of A, B + D troops on relieved were collected at bridge 24 under Bn arrangements and sent up on lorries to DAMBRE CAMP. The remainder of the Bn were relieved on the night 28/29 when Capt Lloyd, 2 Lt Burke and 90 OR. returned also by lorries from the CANAL. During operations communication was maintained throughout by Lucas lamp from MON. OU HIBOU. to the BUND at ALBERTA and took in circle from ALBERTA to 6th Canadian Post by telephone and power buzzer. Wire and power buzzer from MON. O.U. HIBOU to ALBERTA were impossible to maintain on account of shell fire. The camp at the BUND was annoyed by the enemy from about V 25 and was also shelled. About the same time on the 28 we were relieved through of the 58th Div arrived near the front line to relieve this division. It was noticed they were carrying full marching order. A most extraordinary thing —

WAR DIARY
or
INTELLIGENCE SUMMARY.
(Erase heading not required.)

Army Form C. 2118.

Place	Date	Hour	Summary of Events and Information	Remarks and references to Appendices
			The provision of the lorries was a very great saving to the troops, the camp were just shelters and the troops had a good meal. On the 29th the Bn had just come out of the line went by lorry to Select Camp nr. TAMSTER, BISEZEN. The remainder entrained at VLAMIERTINHE detrained at POPERINGHE and marched to SCHOUR CAMP. Here a number of the Bn from the CORPS REINFORCEMENT CAMP rejoined. The following were mentioned by their Corps Commander for gallantry and devotion to duty:—	
			A Coy 41349 Pte R. NOVIS. 41355 Pte R QUINN. 200 654 Sergt. S. COOPER.	
			B Coy 200601 Sergt. R ANNAN.	
			C Coy 200132 L/C M. WEAVER.	
			D Coy 200445 C.S.M. Wm SHAKESPEARE 201047 C/S F. GREEN 200671 S/S E. SNIEYD 201180 Pte E. BOND 200268 Pte A. PROTHEROE (Stretcher Bearer)	

WAR DIARY
or
INTELLIGENCE SUMMARY.

Casualties during the operations 26/25 are as follows:

Officers — 6.
- Capt. J.R. Wallace M.C. — Killed
- Capt. P. Carter M.C. ⎫
- Capt. A.O. Lloyd M.C. ⎬ wounded.
- 2nd Lt. R.R. Thomson ⎭
- 2nd Lt. W.F. Biggs Walker ⎦
- Capt. A.H. Butcher was wounded and remained on duty.

Other Ranks:
- Killed — 21
- Wounded — 68
- Missing — 7

Wounded but remained on duty — 3

Total Other Ranks — 99

J.W. Tomkinson Lieut. Col.
Comdg. 1/7th Bn. Worcestershire Regt.

M-31

Correspondence 14/8 Vol 31

War Diary
of
1/1st Bn the Worcestershire Regiment TF

From 1st to 30th September 1914

(XXX)
(Vol 704)

Army Form C. 2118.

WAR DIARY
or
INTELLIGENCE SUMMARY.
(Erase heading not required.)

Instructions regarding War Diaries and Intelligence Summaries are contained in F. S. Regs., Part II. and the Staff Manual respectively. Title pages will be prepared in manuscript.

Place	Date	Hour	Summary of Events and Information	Remarks and references to Appendices
SCHOOLS CAMP St. JANSTER DIEZEN	1-9-17		Baths in POPERINGHE. Clean Clothing Supplied – Baths-Dries at 6 P.M.	
do	2-9-17		Voluntary Church Services. Actg. Capt. N. O. Shay & Warrant Offr b M.C.	
do	3-9-17		Inspection of Arms by Brunnet Armour Sgt. Lewis Gun Class-Class adopted 30" Range for Shown work.	
do	4-9-17		Coys at disposal of OC Coys for Platoon Coy training. Caufbourdens by E.A. officers.	
do	5-9-17		Coys at Lettie Range. All gas appearance inspected by Div Gas Offr Ryan "Good"	
do	6-9-17		Coys at disposal of OC Coy for training. Inspection of Bn by C.O. at 6.30pm Stepper by rams. Coys & Lewis Gun inspected. Inspection of Transport by OC Bn Train. Report "Very good". Coys at Lettie Range. Remaining loss of inspection by C.O.	
do	7-9-17			
do	8-9-17		Coys at disposal of OC Coys for Route March and 1 hour physical training & inspection by Div Armourer. Honors Awarded. BAR to M.M. 200671 Cpl G. SNYED. MM 413499 Pte B. NOVIS. 200768 Pte A. PROTHERO. G.O.C presented Football Cap & Medals to Players.	

Army Form C. 2118.

WAR DIARY
INTELLIGENCE SUMMARY
(Erase heading not required.)

Place	Date	Hour	Summary of Events and Information	Remarks and references to Appendices
Sch: Hools Camp St Jansten Bizen	9.9.17		Voluntary Church Service. Bn paraded for inspection by Capt SNYED R.C. & Rev R.J. Thur.	
	10.9.17		All officers W.O.s & N.C.O.s given a demonstration of a new attack formation. Coys at bayonet & on the bat for bayonet fighting. Platoons drill & bbo. Coys Arcl.	
	11.9.17		Coys practise attack formation. own fire on Range.	
	12.9.17		Coy on Range.	
	13.9.17		Coys as disposed of. Or Coys Inspection attack formations.	
	14.9.17		Coys on Range. Coys on Route march & rifle.	
	15.9.17		Coys on Bayonet & Or Coys for training. Subject Close order drill. Bayonet fighting.	
	16.9.17		Voluntary Church Service. Transport proceeding by road to Rwe ABEELE off at 9-45 am. Bn to HELLES AREA. Bn paraded at 2.00pm and marched to ABEELE Stn & entrained at 5-30pm. Trains late, did not arrive until 1am 18th. Spent interval in billets. Marching but only very slight shown.	
Zutkerque 18.9.17			Entrained at ABEELE 1am arrived AUDRICQ 9am marched to "BELL" Camp 3 miles. Att in 11 Am for Billet inspection.	
do.	19.9.17		Bn paraded at 7-10 Am to take part in Brigade Tactical exercise on "B" AREA W/N OF DRUQUE. All in at 8pm.	

Army Form C. 2118.

WAR DIARY
or
INTELLIGENCE SUMMARY.
(Erase heading not required.)

Instructions regarding War Diaries and Intelligence Summaries are contained in F. S. Regs., Part II. and the Staff Manual respectively. Title pages will be prepared in manuscript.

Place	Date	Hour	Summary of Events and Information	Remarks and references to Appendices
ZUTKERQUE	20/9/17			
do.	21/9/17		Batln. less "D" Coy carried out SCHEME "A" on their firing Range at GUEMY.- Coys to fire on B RANGE at the following hours D.Cy 2-30 pm C Cy-3-30 pm B Cy 4-30 pm A Cy 5-30 pm	
do.	22/9/17		Coys at disposal of OC Coys for inclement weather and Training. No training owing to rain.	
do.	23/9/17		D Coy carried out SCHEME "A" on GUEMY field firing Range - Volunteer Church Lappen	
do.	24/9/17		Coys at disposal of OC Coys for Training	
"	25/9/17		D Coy attacked the Battn in DIVISIONAL Competition SCHEME "A" was offensive in Competition 5th. Other Coys at disposal of OC Coys for Training	Pure
"	26/9/17		Coys at disposal of OC Coys for Training. 6 inches wearing the B.D.E Respirator for 1/2 hour during Musketry Instruction.	
"	27/9/17		Bn. paraded in fighting order at 7-45 A.m. to take part in Bde. Exercise ROUTHEE or B. AREA. Returned to Billets at 4 p.m.	
"	28/9/17		Coys at disposal of OC Coys for Training. Brigade attack on nunnie windnies 300 SE of Bn HQ turn.	
"	29/9/17		Coys at disposal of OC Coys for Training. Transport proceeding by Road to new AREA left at 7-25 A.m.	

Army Form C. 2118.

WAR DIARY
INTELLIGENCE SUMMARY.
(Erase heading not required.)

Place	Date	Hour	Summary of Events and Information	Remarks and references to Appendices
ZUTKERQUE	30th		Entrained at AUDRICQ for BRAKEEAMP	floor
			Casualties for the month.	
			1 OR wounded and Remained at Duty.	
	30/9/17			

Inspection. Must be
Comdg 17 Bn The Lincolnshire Regt.

Confidential

"17th" Worcestershire Regiment

WAR DIARY

1st October – 31st October 1917

VOLUME XXXI

Army Form C. 2118.

WAR DIARY
or
INTELLIGENCE SUMMARY.
(Erase heading not required.)

Instructions regarding War Diaries and Intelligence Summaries are contained in F. S. Regs., Part II. and the Staff Manual respectively. Title pages will be prepared in manuscript.

Place	Date	Hour	Summary of Events and Information	Remarks and references to Appendices
FLANDERS	1914			
ZUTKERQUE	Oct 1st	4 am	"A" Company left billets at ZUTKERQUE and marched to AUDRICQ Station, entrained for VLAMERTIGNE, proceeding on arrival to REIGERSBURG Camp. They found a working party of 2 officers and 100 O.R. for working on buried cables in the vicinity of SPOT FARM	
		5 am	"D" Coy left their billets and marched to AUDRICQ Stn finding a loading party of 2 officers & 100 O.R. They left for VLAMERTIGNE at 3 pm. Battn Hqrs and "B" & "C" Coys received orders to stand by ready to move on 2 hours notice	
		9.30 am	Orders received to march to AUDRICQ Station to entrain	
		11 am	Reached station and bivouaced in a field adjoining the station	
		12 Dn.	"D" Coy reached billets in BRAKE CAMP A.30 central	
	Oct 2.	12.40am	Bn Hqrs, B & C Coys entrained for VLAMERTIGNE arriving there at 8.30 am, and marched to BRAKE CAMP.	
			A Company found working party of 2 officers & 100 O.R. for work near SPOT FARM	
VLAMERTIGNE AREA	Oct 3		Companies at the disposal of O.C. Companies for training.	

Army Form C. 2118.

WAR DIARY
or
INTELLIGENCE SUMMARY.
(Erase heading not required.)

Instructions regarding War Diaries and Intelligence Summaries are contained in F. S. Regs., Part II. and the Staff Manual respectively. Title pages will be prepared in manuscript.

Place	Date	Hour	Summary of Events and Information	Remarks and references to Appendices
	1917			
BRAKE CAMP	Oct 3	8 am	"A" Company marched in from REIGERSBURG CAMP	
	Oct 4		Batt. Working party of 1 Offr + 50 OR for MADEL. Two platoons of D Coy reported to O.C. Advanced Dressing Station for work there.	
		11 AM	Orders received to stand by ready to move at one hours notice. We did not move.	
	Oct 5	2 pm	Marched to billets in DAMBRE CAMP, VLAMERTIGNE where the two platoons of D Coy rejoined the battalion	
DAMBRE CAMP	Oct 6		Companies at the disposal of O.C. Coys.	
	Oct 7	9 am	Moved to dugout billets in CANAL BANK, north of YPRES.	
	" 8		Battn paraded in fighting order, and took over the right front of the 13 BDE Sector of the line from the 1/4 Royal Berkshire Regt. Weather very bad.	
	Oct 9		The Battn moved into position of assembly E of the STEENBEEK for an attack on ADLER FM, INCH HOUSE, VARLET FM, and WALLEMOLEN. Order of Coys:- B on Right Front with ADLER HOUSE as objective. C Coy on left Front with Trench N of ADLER FM as objective. A Coy. Right Support with	

Army Form C. 2118.

WAR DIARY
or
INTELLIGENCE SUMMARY.
(Erase heading not required.)

Place	Date	Hour	Summary of Events and Information	Remarks and references to Appendices
YPRES AREA	9th (cont)		WALLEMOLEN as objective. D Coy left Support with VARLET FM as objective.	
		2 am	All in Position. Zero fixed for 5.20 a.m.	
		5.20 am	Barrage came down & companies moved forward in order given.	
			The attack was held up by rifle and machine gun fire, but eventually got forward, taking ADLER FM and TRENCH to N. but failed to take final objectives.	
			Casualties during the action:-	
			Officers O.R.	
			Killed 5 54.	
			Wounded 5 135.	
			Wounded at Duty — 1	
			Missing — 22	
			Total 10 212.	
			Complete Report of Action with Operation Orders attached.	

Army Form C. 2118.

WAR DIARY
or
INTELLIGENCE SUMMARY.
(Erase heading not required.)

Instructions regarding War Diaries and Intelligence Summaries are contained in F. S. Regs., Part II. and the Staff Manual respectively. Title pages will be prepared in manuscript.

Place	Date	Hour	Summary of Events and Information	Remarks and references to Appendices
YPRES AREA	Oct 10		The battalion was relieved by the 7th Seaforth Highlanders of the Royal on the night Oct. 10/11 and moved back to SIEGE CAMP.	
	" 11	11 am	All reported in camp. Remained at SIEGE CAMP.	
	" 12		Moved to SCHOOLS CAMP, ST JAN STER BIEZEN.	
		6.45 pm	All reported in camp.	
	" 13		Remained at SCHOOLS CAMP.	
LENS AREA	Oct 14	1.45 AM	Moved to 1st ARMY area. Battn entrained at HOPOUTRE for LIGNY ST FLOCHEL.	
LIGNY ST FLOCHEL		10 AM	Detrained at LIGNY and marched to billets at AUBIGNY.	
		5 pm	All reported in billets.	
	" 16		Marched to billets at VILLERS AU BOIS. Seven men fell out on the march. All reported in at 10 pm.	
VILLERS AU BOIS	" 16		Corps at the disposal of O.C. Corps	
NEUVILLE ST VAAST	Oct 17		Relieved the 31st Canadian Battalion as Brigade Reserve. Relief reported complete at 5 pm.	

Army Form C. 2118.

WAR DIARY
or
INTELLIGENCE SUMMARY.
(Erase heading not required.)

Instructions regarding War Diaries and Intelligence Summaries are contained in F. S. Regs., Part II. and the Staff Manual respectively. Title pages will be prepared in manuscript.

Place	Date	Hour	Summary of Events and Information	Remarks and references to Appendices
NEUVILLE ST VAAST	Oct 18		Brigade Reserve. Coys working on Camp Improvement	
	" 19		Brigade Reserve	
	" 20		Brigade Reserve	
VIMY	" 21	4.35pm	Battalion moved forward to Brigade Support in relief of 1/6 Bn Gloucestershire Regt.	
		8.15pm	Relief reported complete. Working Parties:- 3 officers 150 OR for trench work on HAYTER TR. 3 hours work commenced at 8.30pm.	
			2 officers 50 OR as carrying party for 6th Gloucesters in line	
	" 22		Support Bn. Working Parties:- 3 offrs 150 OR for work on HAYTER TR. 3 hours work to commence at 5.30pm.	
			Casualties by Shell fire :- One.	
			1 officer 50 OR as carrying party for Forward Battn. Report 5.45 pm.	
	" 23		Support Battn. A and C Coys changed places. B & D Coys changed places. 3 hrs wk. 5.30pm. Works :- 3 officers 150 OR for work on HAYTER TR.	

Army Form C. 2118.

WAR DIARY
or
INTELLIGENCE SUMMARY.

(Erase heading not required.)

Instructions regarding War Diaries and Intelligence Summaries are contained in F. S. Regs., Part II. and the Staff Manual respectively. Title pages will be prepared in manuscript.

Place	Date	Hour	Summary of Events and Information	Remarks and references to Appendices
	1917.			
VIMY.	Sept 23 contd		1 Officer 50 O.R. carrying party for Forward Battn. Report 5.45 p.m. Support Battn. Working Parties:-	
	Oct 24.		1 Off. 150 O.R. working on KEANE T.R. 1 Officer and 30 O.R. carrying for Forward Battn.	
	" 25		Relieved 1/6 Bn Gloucester Regt as Outpost Battn. Relief commenced 5.45 p.m. and reported complete 9.0 p.m. Line held "A" Coy on Right, B Coy Right Centre, C Coy Left Centre, D Coy Left.	
	" 26		Trenches. Enemy attempted a raid on our left Coy at 12.45 a.m., the was beaten off leaving 1 dead, and 4 rifles. Our casualties:- Capt P. Carter MC wounded, 6 O.R. wounded.	
	" 27		Trenches	
	" 28		Trenches	
	" 29		Trenches, relieved by 1/8 Worcestershire Regt. Relief commenced 6 p.m. Complete at 9 p.m. On relief Bn went into camp as follows.	
NEUVILLE			A Coy: HILLS CAMP, B Coy: CELLAR CAMP, C+D Coy: HQrs	
ST VAAST.			in CUBITTS CAMP. All in at 1 a.m.	

Army Form C. 2118.

WAR DIARY
or
INTELLIGENCE SUMMARY.
(Erase heading not required.)

Place	Date	Hour	Summary of Events and Information	Remarks and references to Appendices
NEUVILLE ST VAAST	Oct 30		A&B Coy. provided Working Party of 2 Offrs 200 O.R. to work on CELLAR & HUTS CAMPS.	
MT ST ELOI	31	3.30pm	HQrs, C & D Coys. moved to OTTAWA CAMP MT ST. ELOI. Left in S 20th and C & D Coys at disposal of OC Corp. A&B Coy. Party of 2 Offrs 200 men for Camp Building.	
			Monthly Total Casualties	
			K. W. M.	
			3 O.R.	
			Oct 2. A Coy. -- 6 -- 3 W. remain on duty	
			" 5 D " 1 18 -	
			" 9/11 A " 11 28 4	
			B " 12 37 9	Officers K.W. 5 5 (1 since died)
			C " 13 51 3	
			D "	
			Oct 13 B " 1 1 (Rem on Duty)	
			" 22nd C " 1	
			" 27 D " 6 9 1 Officer Wounded.	

M W Arbuthnot Major.
Commanding
1/7 Bn the Worcestershire Regt

The following is a table of the casualties sustained during the operations:-

Officers — 2nd Lt. P.P. EDWARDS (C Coy) } Killed in action
2nd Lt. D.M. LEWIS (C Coy) }

Capt. G.G. WATSON (D Coy)
Capt. W.R. PRESCOTT M.C. (B Coy) } Wounded
2nd Lt. D.O. LITTLE M.C. (D Coy)
2nd Lt. H.J. CAMPBELL (C Coy)

Other Ranks

	Killed in action	Wounded	Missing	Wounded (Remained to Duty)	Total Casualties
A Coy		5			5
B Coy	5	15	3	1	24
C Coy	8	44	6	2	60
D Coy	5	29	10	2	46
	18	93	19	5	135

www.ingramcontent.com/pod-product-compliance
Lightning Source LLC
Chambersburg PA
CBHW081531160426
43191CB00011B/1737